Grimacing gargoyles adorn many of the churches in Leicestershire and Rutland. Alongside them are a wide range of imaginary beasties, foliate faces, 'Green Men', face-pulling heads, contortionists, and other imaginative figurative carvings. While those on the outside of the churches may be badly weathered, their counterparts inside are usually near-perfect examples of the medieval mason's skills.

Leicestershire and Rutland are fortunate in having more such carvings than adjoining counties, although this wealth of medieval art has been unjustly overlooked by church historians. These depictions provide a unique insight into the often rather disturbing thinking of the craftsmen who carved them many hundreds of years ago, people who are otherwise almost entirely invisible from historical records.

The aim of the *Good Gargoyle Guide* is to encourage people who would not normally take an interest in church architecture to get out and about hunting further examples of these extraordinary sculptures.

Bob Trubshaw has been researching Leicestershire and Rutland medieval carvings for over eighteen years. The first edition of the *Good Gargoyle Guide* was published in 1991.

Good Gargoyle Guide

Medieval carvings of Leicestershire and Rutland

Bob Trubshaw

Heart of Albion Press

Good Gargoyle Guide
Medieval carvings of Leicestershire and Rutland
2nd edition 2004

Bob Trubshaw

Cover illustration: Lowesby church tower by Bob Trubshaw

ISBN 1 872883 70 2

1st edition published by Heart of Albion Press 1991.
Text and images based on *Interactive Gargoyles and Grotesque Carvings of Leicestershire and Rutland* CD-ROM published by Heart of Albion Press 2002.

Heart of Albion Press
2 Cross Hill Close, Wymeswold
Loughborough, LE12 6UJ

albion@indigogroup.co.uk

Visit our Web site: www.hoap.co.uk

Printed in the UK by Booksprint

Contents

Acknowledgements

Permission to reproduce photographs has been kindly granted by relevant clergy in Rutland; Heritage Services Leicestershire County Council (the roof boss now in Market Harborough Museum); Bob Jarrett (Appleby Magna carvings); Carole Law (all carvings in or on churches in Leicester Diocese); Rutland County Museum (Oakham Castle corbel); and Ruth Wylie (green men at Buckminster and Sileby).

Over the years many friends have shared 'church crawling' expeditions and added to the enjoyment. Joan Shaw made numerous suggestions for improving the version of this survey published as *Interactive Gargoyles and Grotesque Carvings of Leicestershire and Rutland.* Paul Nix has provided essential technical support for many years. My grateful thanks to all.

You will also need...

To navigate around Leicestershire and Rutland the relevant Ordnance Survey 1:50,000 maps are essential. Ordnance Survey grid references provided in this guide are for the church. They are prefixed with the relevant OS map number.

Serious 'church crawlers' will want to have a copy of Nikolaus Pevsner's *Leicestershire and Rutland* (Penguin, 1984). Also useful is the National Association of Decorative and Fine Arts Societies' guide to church furnishings, *Inside churches* (Capability Publishing, 1989).

A pair of binoculars will help greatly when studying many of these carvings.

While I fully appreciate the need to keep churches locked, I have nothing polite to say about the parishes where no information on current key holders is visible (and, in these days of mobile phones, key holders' phone numbers are much more helpful than addresses). If your interest in carvings means you will want to attempt to see inside most of the churches then I suggest you obtain copies of the current Diocesan Directories from the Diocesan Offices in Leicester (phone number at time of going to print 0116 248 7400) and, for Rutland churches, Peterborough Diocese (phone number at time of going to print 01733 887000). These contain up to date addresses and phone numbers for all clergy and churchwardens; both are moderately priced.

Glossary

Art historians revel in creating 'typologies' and obscure terminology as a short-hand among themselves but which are more-or-less meaningless to the uninitiated. Sadly these terms are often used willy-nilly in church guide books by writers who, presumably seeking to impress others with their erudition, succeed instead in perplexing visitors. In case you come across them, here is a summary of the frequently used terms used to refer to the succession of different decorative styles.

Anglo-Saxon	600–1066
Romanesque (Norman)	1066–1180
Transitional	1175–1200
Early English (Gothic)	1190–1250
Geometric (Gothic)	1250–1290
Decorated (Gothic)	1290–1350
Perpendicular (Gothic)	1325–1530
Tudor	1485–1603
Baroque	C17–18
Queen Anne	early C18
Georgian (Neoclassical)	1714–1830
Gothic Revival	C19
Arts and Crafts	1860s to early C20

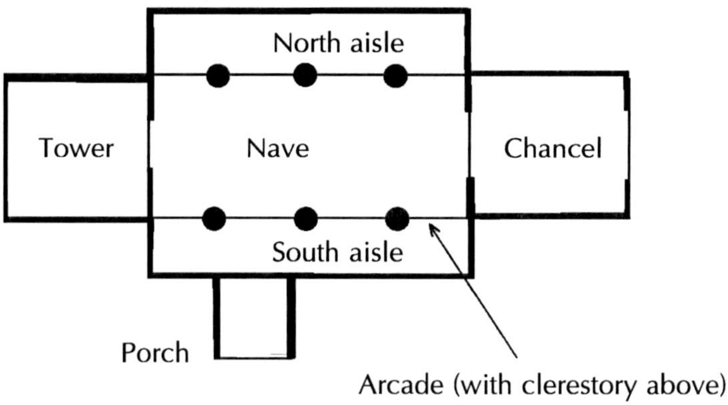

Schematic plan of a typical Rutland church. See Glossary for a more detailed explanation of terms used.

aisle: used here not to refer to the central walkway in the **nave** but to the extensions on the north and/or south sides of the nave, separated by **arcades**.

arcade: A series of arches on columns or piers, usually between the **nave** and the **aisles**.

aumbry: a small cupboard built into the wall of the chancel for storing the chalice and other liturgical vessels.

bellcote: An open structure on which the bells are hung, sometimes known as a bell turret. Twin bellcotes are especially common on Rutland churches.

box pew: Enclosed seating, often with doors, usually dating from the seventeenth or eighteenth century. They often were reserved for the use of specific families. Victorian church restorers were keen to remove these and replace them with 'open' pews.

broach: an octagonal spire merged into a square tower with triangular 'facets'.

capitals: the large blocks on top of a column or pillar, directly beneath the arch. They are often decorated, sometimes with stylised foliage, occasionally with figures or other more elaborated motifs.

chancel: the eastern part of a church, otherwise known as the choir.

clerestory: windows high up in the **nave**. They are often more recent than the rest of the nave, becoming very fashionable in the fifteenth century.

corbels: blocks of masonry partially set into walls and originally supporting roof timbers (although many are now functionless if the roof height has been raised).

crockets: rows of hook-like or leaf-like projections, usually on the edges of a spire.

foliate face: a face surrounded by leaves, or where the features are formed from leaves.

frieze: Fairly self-explanatory — a continuous band of decorative carving with, usually, rather small figures of faces, animals or vegetation. One distinctive style of flower is very stylised and known as ball flower.

gargoyle: To be found on the outside of churches, around the tower and along the nave and aisle roofs. 'Gargoyle' is a term often used indiscriminately for any grotesque carving; I use it in its strict sense of a carving designed to drain rain-water off the roof away from the walls. (The word 'gargoyle' derives from the Old French word *gargouille* meaning 'throat'; the word 'gargle' shares the same origin.)

green man: a foliate face where branches sprout from the mouth, nose or eyes.

girning or **gurning:** pulling a face by putting one or both hands in the mouth and then grimacing.

hagioscope —see 'squint'

ha-ha: a wall above a ditch, preventing animals entering a park or garden without interrupting the view when seen from the house.

hatchment: a coat of arms hung in the church after a person's death.

label stop: the technical term for where the arch of a window or doorway meets the vertical sides.

lucarne: a narrow opening with a dormer-like gabled top, usually in a spire.

mass dial —see 'scratch dial'

nave: the part of the church where the congregation sit.

pilaster: a rectangular column projecting from a wall.

piscina: washing basin for the chalice and other sacred vessels, often richly carved.

reredos: an ornamental screen covering the wall behind an altar.

roof bosses: decorative carving along the centre of a roof.

rood loft: a 'platform' above the rood screen separating the nave and chancel. In medieval times this platform would have supported sculptures of the 'rood' i.e. Jesus on the cross, together with sculptures of the Virgin Mary and St John the Baptist. Almost without exception the rood lofts have gone, leaving only a set of twisting stairs that once provided access.

rood screen: a carved screen separating the nave and chancel.

scratch dial: Simple sundials to assist the clergy to assess the time of the Offices of the liturgy were apparently once common on the south side of churches. These are known as either 'scratch dials' or 'mass dials'. Unfortunately, both these names are misleading —the carving (at least on those that have survived!) is much deeper than a mere 'scratch'. But 'mass dial' is even more misleading as Mass was celebrated rarely before the mid-nineteenth century (perhaps only once or twice a year); the daily and weekly liturgy revolved around the Offices (such as matins and vespers). For lack of a better alternative, I refer to them as scratch dials.

Typically scratch dials are situated on the wall near to where the priest entered, so sometimes they are by the south porch; where there is a priest's door direct into the chancel the scratch dial may be there instead. The lines radiate from a small hole (where a stick would have been inserted); curiously so lines radiate above as well as below the centre, although this is apparently redundant effort!

Where multiple scratch dials are found at the same church the radiating lines are usually differently spaced. They may be 'winter' and 'summer' alternatives, or simply reflect the changing preferences of successive clergy.

sedilia: seats built into the wall, often in the form of beautifully carved niches. Usually there are three, one each for the priest, deacon and sub-deacon who assisted with the liturgy. The three seats are often ranked, with the tallest nearest the altar.

squint: a hole or window through the masonry that enabled priests at side altars to see the main altar, so that key events of the Mass could be synchronised when celebrated simultaneously at the different altars. Also known as a hagioscope.

stoup: a stone basin for holy water.

tympanum: a carved semi-circular stone intended to fill the gap between the door lintel and the arch above.

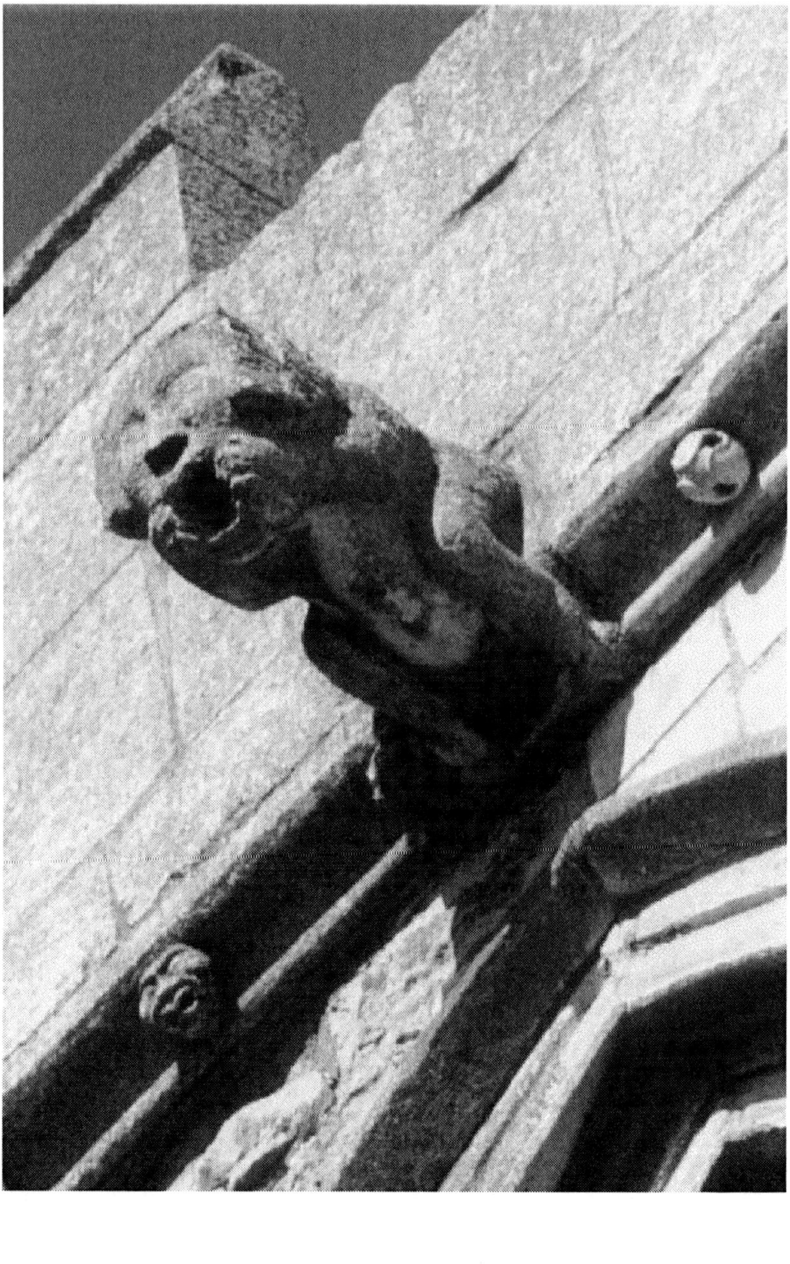

Gurning gargoyle, South Croxton. Note also the ballflower decoration (on right) and a 'matching' human head (on left).

Introduction to carvings

The selection of medieval carvings here does not pretend to be comprehensive —there are many churches in Leicestershire and a few in Rutland that I have not visited. Nor does the information do justice to the many other architectural and ecclesiastical treasures in the counties' churches.

The surviving medieval carvings are often among the best features of the church but the guide books rarely draw attention to them. This is so consistent one begins to suspect a conspiracy of silence among church recorders and historians. Whether deliberate or not, any historian working only from written sources would entirely miss these impressive and widespread carvings and the stories that they continue to tell.

My aim is to draw attention to the wide range of figurative carvings that form an unjustly neglected part of our medieval heritage. Above all, I hope it encourages others, especially those not normally interested in the Church and its buildings, to get out and visit such places.

Brief mention is made of some of the sepulchral effigies and incised slabs. All the effigies in Leicestershire and Rutland churches are described and illustrated in the CD-ROM *Sepulchral Effigies in Leicestershire and Rutland* by Max Wade Matthews (Heart of Albion Press 2002). F. A. Greenhill's *The Incised Slabs of Leicestershire and Rutland* (Leicestershire Archaeological and Historical Society 1958) is an excellent study but sadly long out of print. Incised slabs evolve into commemorative brasses which have been discussed in Dora Valentine's *Church Brasses of Leicestershire* (Vaughan Paper No. 20, University of Leicester, 1975).

How old are these carvings?

The large majority of churches in Leicestershire and Rutland date back to medieval times and visible parts frequently date from the thirteenth and early fourteenth centuries. A surprising number of interesting ancient carvings, mostly in stone but sometimes in wood, have survived both Reformation iconoclasm and heavy-handed restoration. The craftsmanship varies from quaint, clearly local efforts, to sophisticated displays of the stonemasons' skills, with faces and creatures in most animated postures.

There is considerable difficulty in closely dating stone carvings. The same type of tools were used over long periods. External carvings which have begun to erode may be re-cut. Above all, stylistic variations seem to relate primarily to the individual stone-masons. Richard Morris (1989) has argued that changes in fashion in church decoration were transmitted by the masons and, in general, it seems that the masons had considerable control over the details of their activities. I have been informed that masons currently working on the restoration of one of our cathedrals have, by tradition, the right to add whatever decorative motifs they choose. Something of this freedom was expressed when the reconstruction of the south transcept of York Minster in the 1980s incorporated roof bosses designed around themes suggested by a *Blue Peter* competition.

A number of Leicestershire and Rutland churches have traces of Anglo-Saxon or Romanesque carving. However, the majority of the illustrations in this book are of work that is probably thirteenth to fifteenth century. Although similar carvings are fairly common in adjoining parts of Nottinghamshire and Lincolnshire, there is relatively little figurative carving of this age in Warwickshire. Many churches there were restored or rebuilt in the eighteenth century and previous sculpture broken up and incorporated in the walls. The survival of so much medieval carving in Leicestershire and Rutland can be attributed to the relative poverty of these counties in the eighteenth and early nineteenth centuries —there was not enough money to maintain parish churches, let alone rebuild them. (The late eighteenth century illustrations in Nichols reveal that many Leicestershire churches were semi-derelict at the time.)

However from the 1850s widespread church restoration in the 'Gothic revival' style led to many new carvings in a similar style to the original medieval work. As an aside, a number of churches in Leicestershire and Rutland were 'forgotten' by Victorian restorers. Brooke retains an essentially seventeenth century interior while Kings Norton, Stapleford, Teigh and Wistow are all good examples of the quite different fashions for church interiors in the eighteenth century.

One of the worst sins of the Victorian 'restorers' was to remove all traces of original paint from medieval carvings. The evidence of the restorers themselves and coloured prints of the pre-Victorian era show that no medieval carving was complete without a good deal of colour. Indeed, it appears that nearly as much money was spent on the painting and gilding of a sculpture as on its carving (Stone 1955; Brandwood 1990). To imagine these carvings in their original form we need to try to see them not as bare stone but as painted, often in what would now seem garish colour combinations. The backgrounds and faces might be orange ochre with costumes in green highlighted with red ochre. Blue appears to have been less frequently used,

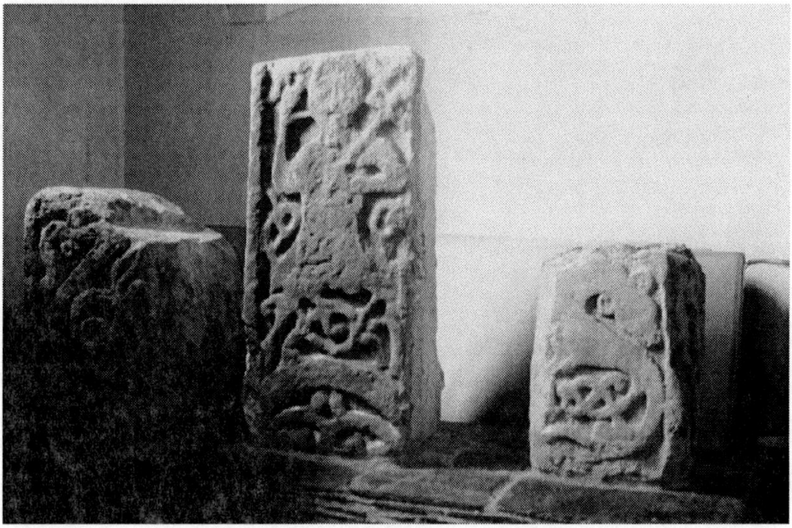

Anglo-Saxon carvings in Asfordby church; note dragon on right.

probably because non-fading pigments were expensive. One of the few churches in Leicestershire where the original colours can be viewed is Ashby Folville. A number of others, notably Lutterworth, have restored their roof bosses to some semblance of the original splendour.

Anglo-Saxon treasures

Strictly many of the 'Anglo-Saxon' carvings in Leicestershire and Rutland should more correctly be referred to as 'Anglo-Scandinavian'. However, purely for convenience, in this introduction I will refer to all styles as Anglo-Saxon.

Leicestershire has one of the best collections of Anglo-Saxon carvings in the country, incorporated into the later churches at Breedon on the Hill. The deeply-carved friezes reveal the skills of a master sculptor. The somewhat stylised saints are accompanied by highly imaginative 'beasties' and geometrical patterns. Elsewhere in Leicestershire and Rutland there are a substantial number of other surviving carvings from this period, mostly fragments from cross shafts. The best examples are at Rothley and Sproxton.

Intriguingly all Leicestershire Anglo-Saxon crosses, except one, are from the same type of stone. This strongly suggests that they were produced at the same place. As with Anglo-Saxon crosses elsewhere

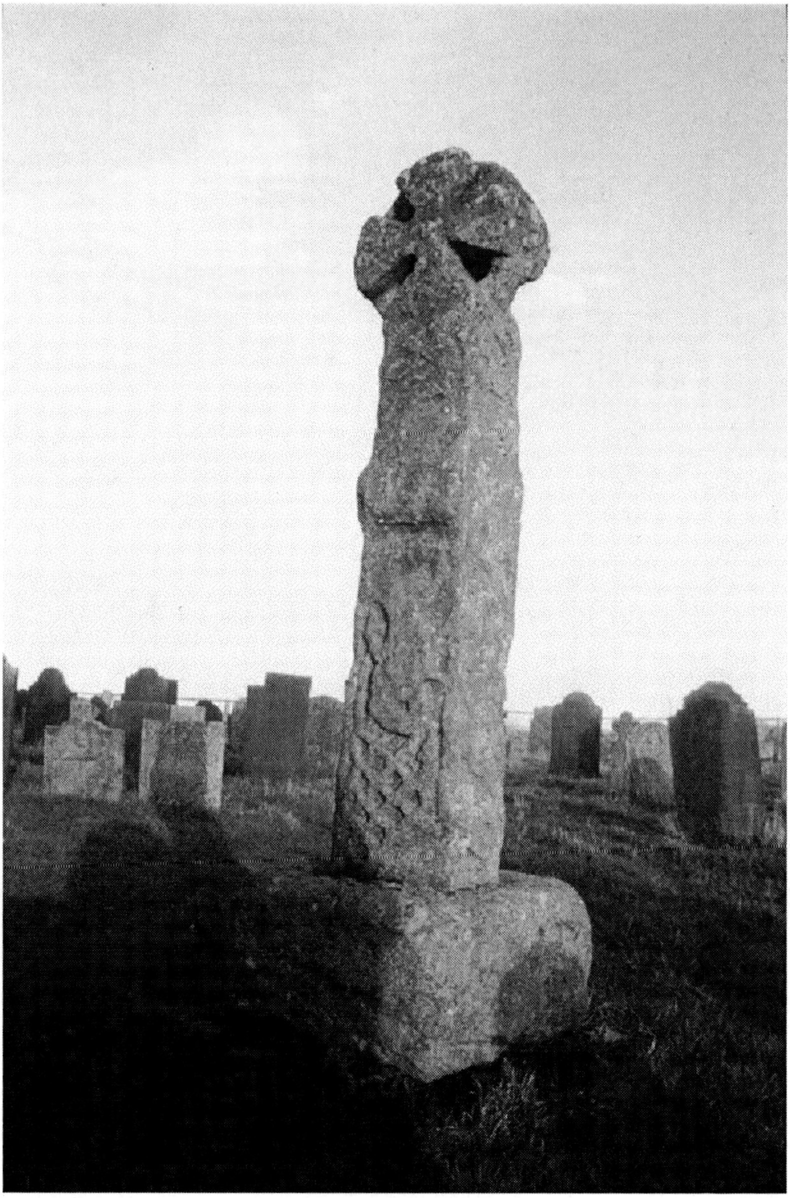

Anglo-Saxon cross shaft at Sproxton. The lower half includes a depiction of a dragon.

in Britain, the sculptors were clearly familiar with styles of decoration used in north-west France (Cloud, no date).

Romanesque exuberance

The Romanesque style is found throughout Western Europe and flourished in the eleventh and twelfth centuries. This more or less approximates to the time of the Norman conquest so in Britain the Romanesque style is widely known as 'Norman architecture' Indeed, the large majority of Romanesque churches in Britain were built in the decades following the conquest of 1066. However, the term 'Norman' is misleading, partly because the earliest examples predate the Norman invasion and, more crucially, because British Romanesque architecture and decoration are part of a style found throughout western Europe, where the Normans had little or no influence.

The Romanesque style made much greater use of decorative carving than the Anglo-Saxons had done previously. Many excellent examples of Romanesque carving still survive in Leicestershire and Rutland.

Romanesque arches and doorways are frequent survivors, although normally only decorated with the characteristic chevron or 'dogs-tooth' ornament.

Romanesque fonts are also plentiful, although many are plain or decorated with architectural arcading, which is supposed to suggest the baptised person entering the Temple of God.

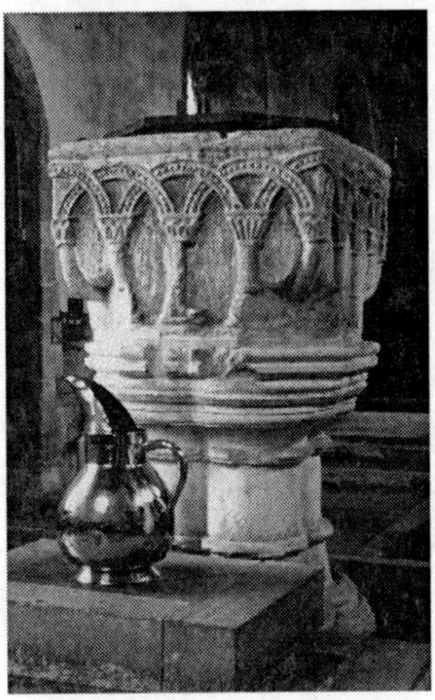

Romanesque font, Foxton.

Tympanums (strictly, the plural is 'tympana') are large blocks of masonry, usually semi-circular, originally fitted over a doorway. They are almost always Romanesque and those that have survived are decorated with carvings.

Beaked heads are a striking but rather obscure motif, usually associated with Romanesque arches. One of the best local examples of beaked head decoration is at Tickencote, and others can be seen on the south doorway of the ruined church of St Mary in Arden, Market Harborough (see photograph on page 7).

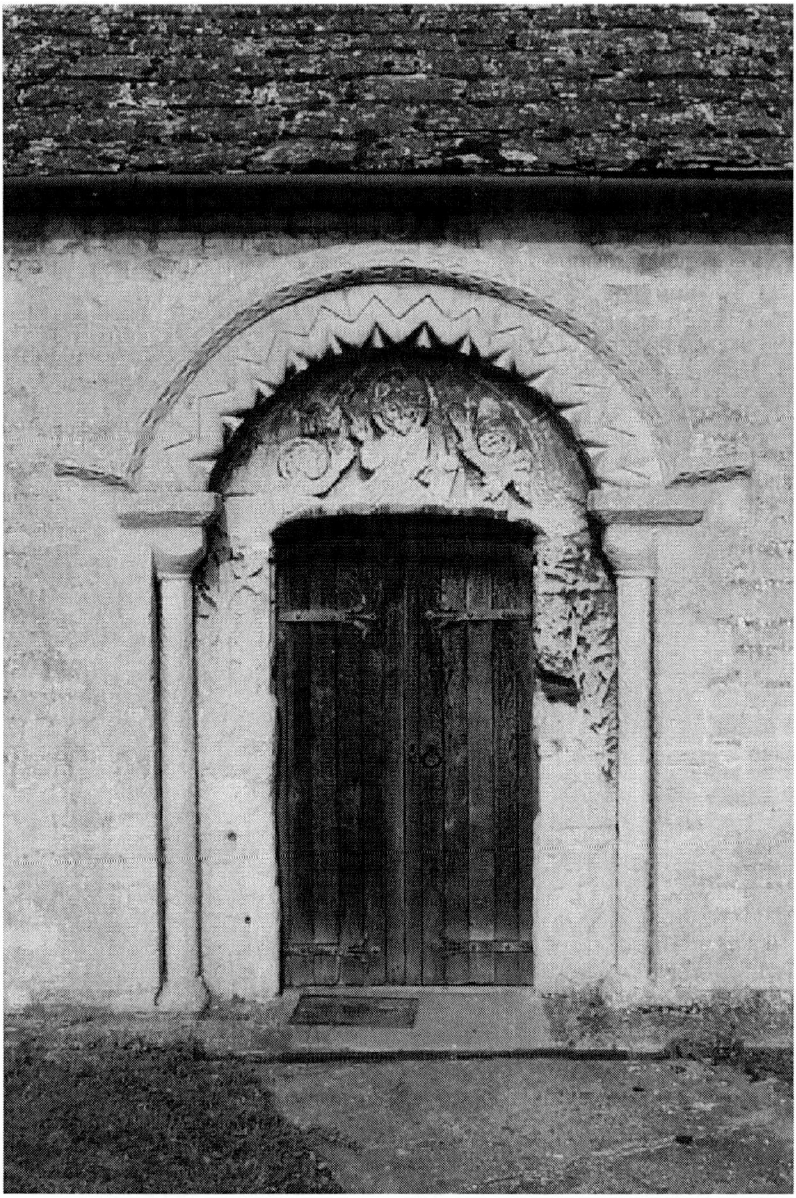

Romanesque doorway and tympanum at Essendine.

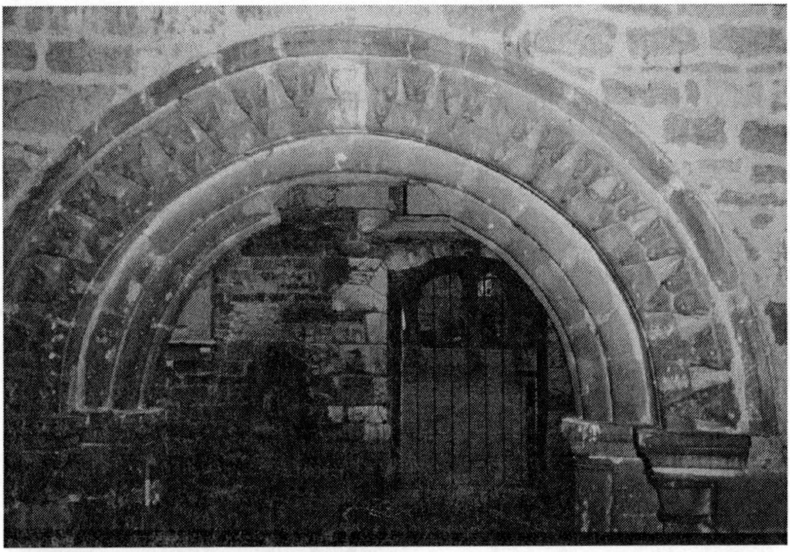

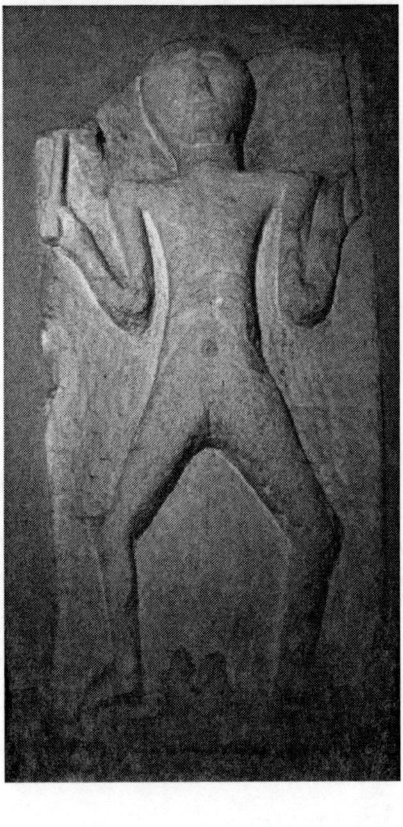

Above: *Beakheads on the Romanesque doorway at St Mary in Arden, Market Harborough.*

Left: *Other Romanesque carvings of note include a figure holding what appears to be a large hammer at Church Langton. Although not a sophisticated piece of carving it does evoke a feeling of power. It is probably from the late eleventh or early twelfth century.*

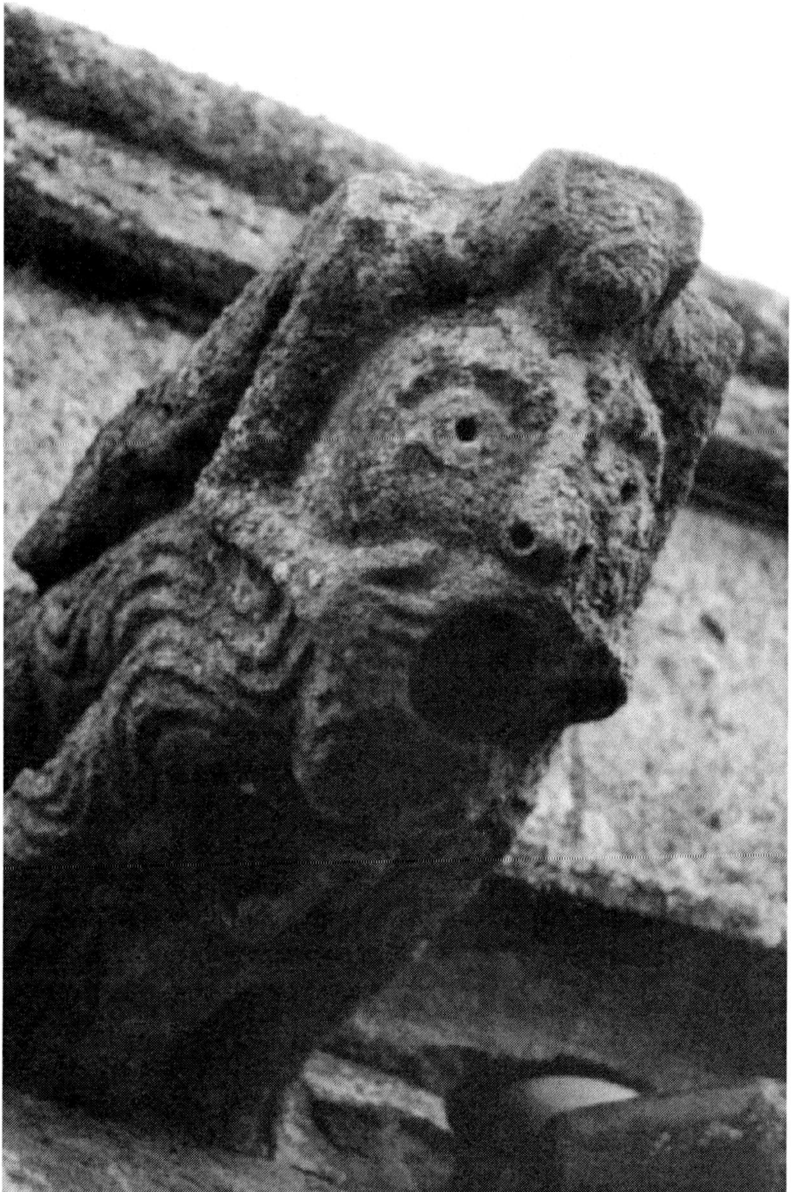

Gargoyle, Loddington church.

Where are these carvings?

There are a few churches, such as Cold Overton, where figurative carving seems to be everywhere. But in most churches there are in predictable places.

On the outside of the church gargoyles may be found around the tower and along the nave and aisle roofs. 'Gargoyle' is a term often used indiscriminately for any grotesque carving; I use it in its strict sense of a carving designed to drain rain-water off the roof away from the walls. (The word 'gargoyle' derives from the Old French word *gargouille* meaning 'throat'; the word 'gargle' shares the same origin.)

Underneath the roof may be a frieze. The name is fairly self-explanatory —a continuous band of decorative carving with, usually, rather small figures of faces, animals or vegetation. One distinctive style of flower is very stylised and known as ball flower, sometimes interspersed with small human heads (see photograph on pxii). Instead of a frieze there may be a series of figurative carvings supporting overhanging stonework; this is known as a 'corbel table'.

Inside look up to where the roof timbers are supported for decorated corbels. Look either side of doors and windows for label stops. Look between arches in the nave arcades for arch springers and decorated capitals. Then look right up at the middle of the roof for bosses.

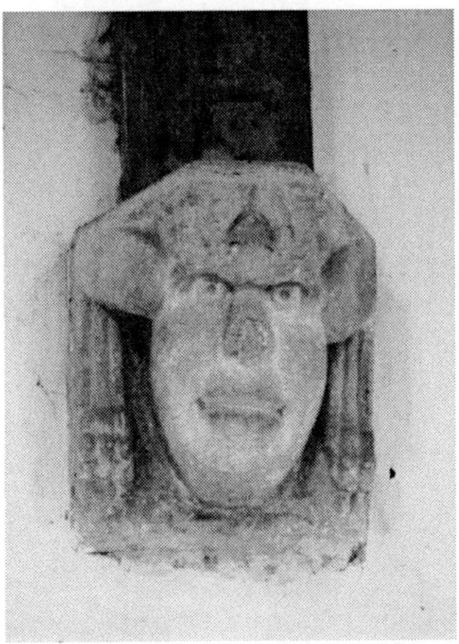

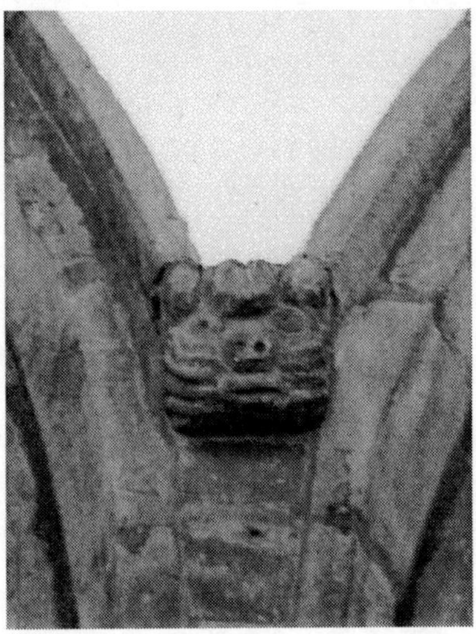

Left: *Corbel, Lyddington church.*
Right: *Springer, Skeffington church.*

Grimacing gargoyles around the roof or tower are, according to more than one church guide, an illustration of how the forces of evil have been banished to the outside of the church. But, if so, why do so many naves and even chancel arches also display corbel heads with similar features?

Just as grotesque gargoyles appear around roofs so faces appear around doorways and windows. These seem to perpetrate an archaic need for protection at liminal places such as entrances. ('Liminal' means literally a 'boundary' or 'threshold' but usually carries the meaning of a place or time which is slightly magical or Otherworldly; see Billingsley 1995, 1998.)

Where the figures form pairs, either side of a doorway or window, it is normal for one to be female and the other male. Done correctly, the male head will be on the left (when viewed from the outside) which matches the position of bride and groom at a Christian wedding.

What do these carvings depict?

These carvings depict human or animal forms in a wonderful variety of styles, from the naturalistic to the grotesque. Some of the more frequent designs include dragons and dragon slayers, green men and foliate faces, gurning faces and tongue pokers.

Less common are such designs as human faces with big 'hare-like' (or ass-like) ears; so-called column-swallowers; and a whole variety of contortionists (frequently 'mooning'). There are various examples of all these in Leicestershire and Rutland, reflecting their widespread but infrequent occurrences throughout Britain.

Dragons and dragon-slayers

Throughout Britain there are many fine depictions of fearsome mythical beasts, sometimes being impaled by more-or-less saintly figures. For convenience I will refer to the victims as dragons, although technically some are wyverns, griffins or merely winged serpents. (What's the difference? Well, these mythical beasts have their own well-defined (un)natural history. Wyverns have a serpent-like body with wings but only two legs; griffins have the upper body of an eagle and the back-end of lion; winged serpents are dragon-like but legless.)

Otherwise quite modest parish churches may contain dragon-slaying sculptures of great artistic and historical interest. Often such carvings are from the Romanesque period although the subject has always remained popular. While the popular Christian exegesis is

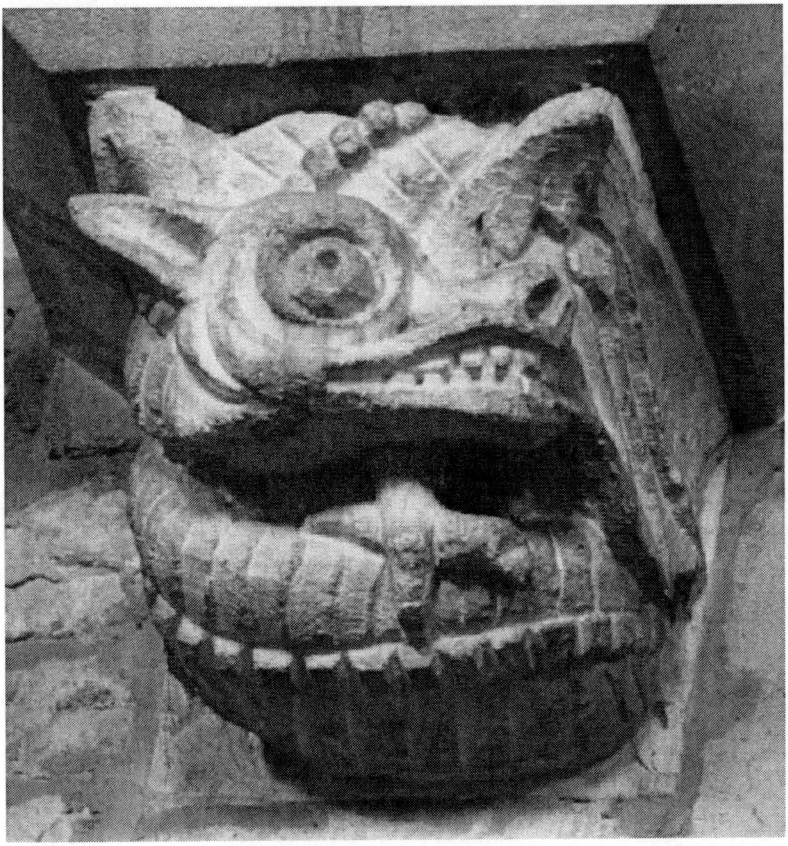

Dragon-like corbel, Sproxton.

that such carvings depict the conquest of Good over Evil, the intention of the Romanesque sculptors appears to be the depiction of a perpetual combat in which there is no victor; so the combatants will remain in contention until the end of time, or at least until the processes of erosion are completed. Only at a much later date do artists depict the saint in a victorious pose over a defunct demon.

Since the medieval era dragons, griffins, wyverns and winged serpents have become ubiquitous heraldic devices and examples are widespread. A 'wyvern' forms the crest of Leicester's heraldic arms. However, Leicester's 'wyvern' is depicted without legs! This was the crest of Thomas, Earl of Lancaster, who was a major landowner in Leicester from 1296 until his execution for treason in 1322. For this reason Leicester's wyvern is often depicted with blood stains. This

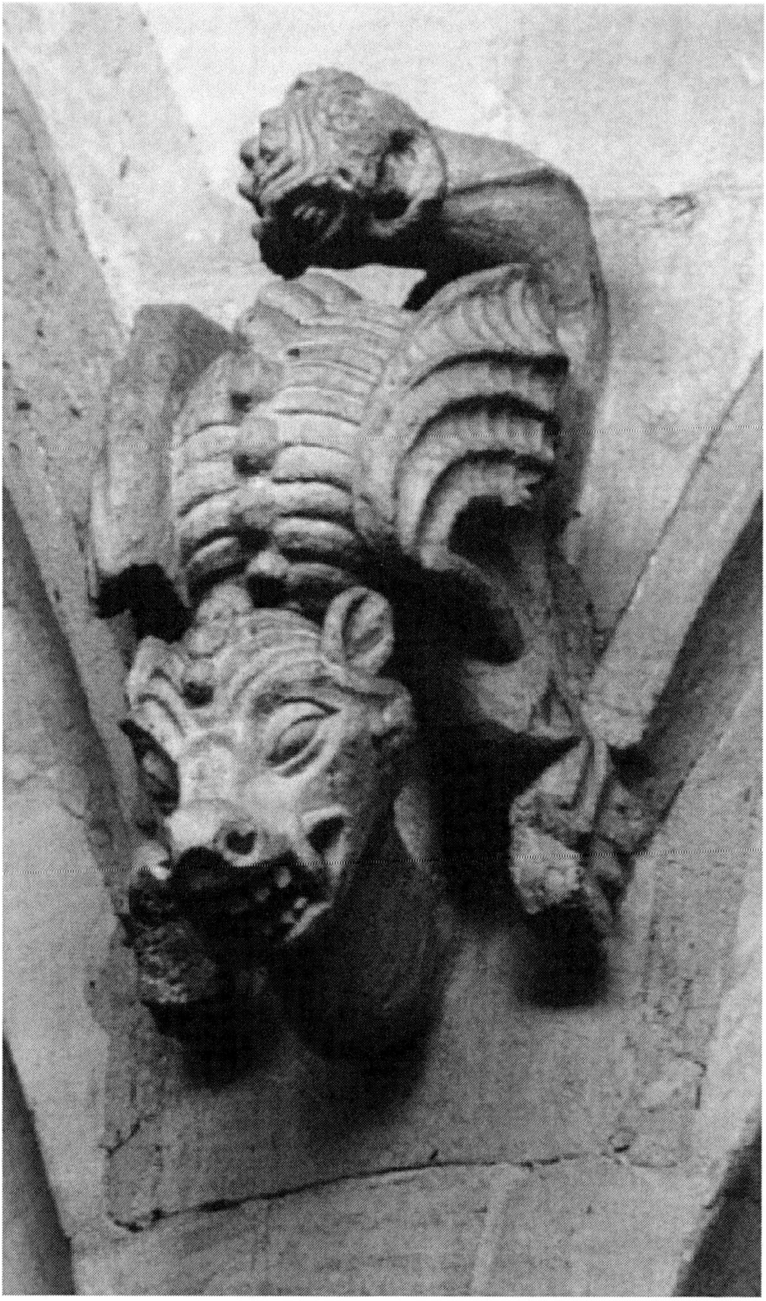

A splendid wyvern in Bottesford church.

'wyvern' appears on many buildings in Leicester including the Town Hall; Phoenix House, Welford Place; Registry Office, Pocklington's Walk; Grand Hotel, Granby Street; Frazer Noble Building, London Road; Clock Tower; Fire Station, Lancaster Road; Cattle Market, Aylestone Road; NatWest Bank, Granby Street; Corn Exchange, Market Place; Freemans Cottages, Welford Road; and (until about 1990, when they were stolen) a pair of wyverns graced the gateposts of the main entrance to Welford Road Cemetery.

Green men and foliate faces

What are green men?

Green men are the one aspect of medieval carving that has gained popular attention in recent years, although the name is often given to foliate faces too. Pedantically, green men have leaves sprouting from their mouth or nose (or, more rarely, their eyes or ears). Foliate faces

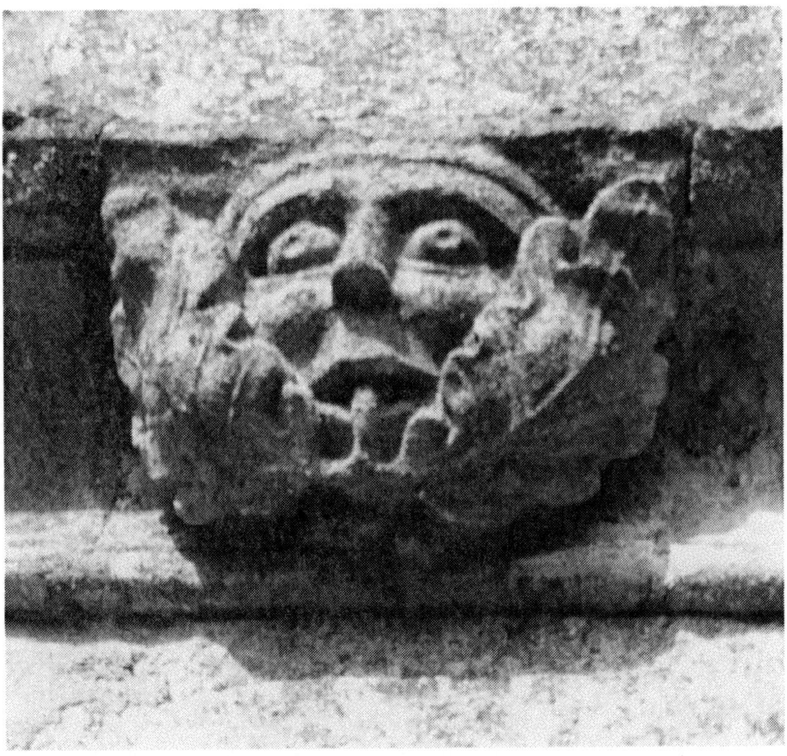

Green Man, Ryhall.

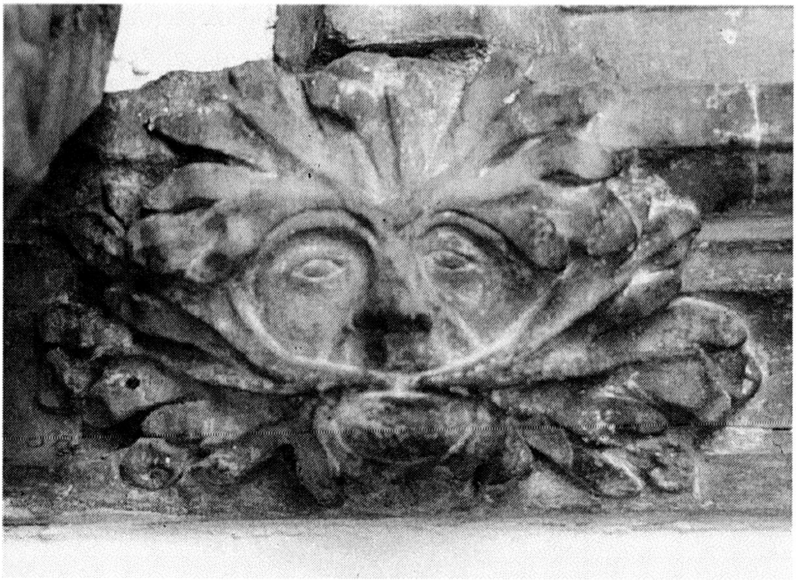

Green man, St Margaret's, Leicester.

can either be relatively naturalistic human or animal faces surrounded by leaves, or can be fanciful faces where the features are all carved in the form of leaves.

In Europe green men date back to the Roman era, although only became widespread during the Romanesque and then becoming even more frequent from the thirteenth century. In her pioneering 1978 study *Green Men* Kathleen Basford noted that the reuse of a Roman capital with a green man motif in the sixth century cathedral at Trier (France) may have provided inspiration for the many masons who visited that building and went on to copy the style elsewhere, culminating in the Romanesque style of the eleventh and twelfth centuries. However more recently Mercia MacDermott has shown that the spouting foliage motif seems to be derived from Indian art imported into Europe in the eleventh century, as exact copies of the Indian motif are included in Romanesque doorways at Moissac (France) and Kilpeck (Herefordshire). For a detailed and up-to-date overview of green men see Dr MacDermott's book, *Explore Green Men* (MacDermott 2003).

There are Romanesque examples of green men in Leicestershire or Rutland at Horninghold, Stoke Dry and Tickencote. Most of the examples of green men depicted in this book probably date from the thirteenth to fifteenth centuries. However the recent revival of interest means that there is a late twentieth century example of a foliate face in at Lyddington.

What green men are not

There is now a strong popular tradition that green men were carved to depict pagan deities of fertility and rebirth. This idea owes its origin to an article by Lady Raglan (1939) and was propounded by various authors, notably William Anderson in his book *The Green Man* (1990) and the closely-linked BBC1 TV programme in November 1990.

However, various academic authors, such as Roy Judge (1979) and Ronald Hutton (1991), conclusively show that the link between medieval green men and pagan fertility gods is an entirely recent invention, not least because the modern distinctions between Christianity and paganism only emerged in the last 150-or-so years.

Anthony Weir and James Jerman (1986) convincingly argue that green men were, in the early Romanesque, part of a series of motifs intended to depict the Seven Deadly Sins (with the green man probably signifying *luxuria* or lust). However, the green man motif seems to have become quickly detached from this original symbolism.

Beyond that, there are few clues as to what green men (or, indeed, any of the other common designs of medieval carvings) signified for the people who carved them. But, despite the now-indelible modern belief, we can be certain that they were *not* intended to depict some prechristian deity or 'spirit'.

Gurning faces

Among the most hideous faces are those which are, literally, pulling faces —with both hands (or occasionally only one) stretching the mouth.

In the north-west of England, face-pulling competitions are still held where the contestants put their heads through a horse collar and pull the most frightening faces possible. These are known as 'gurning championships' and, for convenience, I have adopted this term.

Gurning gargoyles —human and bestial —frequently repose around the roofs of the counties' churches. There are also many excellent examples on the corbels within the nave of churches.

One church guide describes such a figure as 'a man with toothache'. But a less fanciful interpretation is that these faces appear to be a polite version of the sheela-na-gig carvings, otherwise known

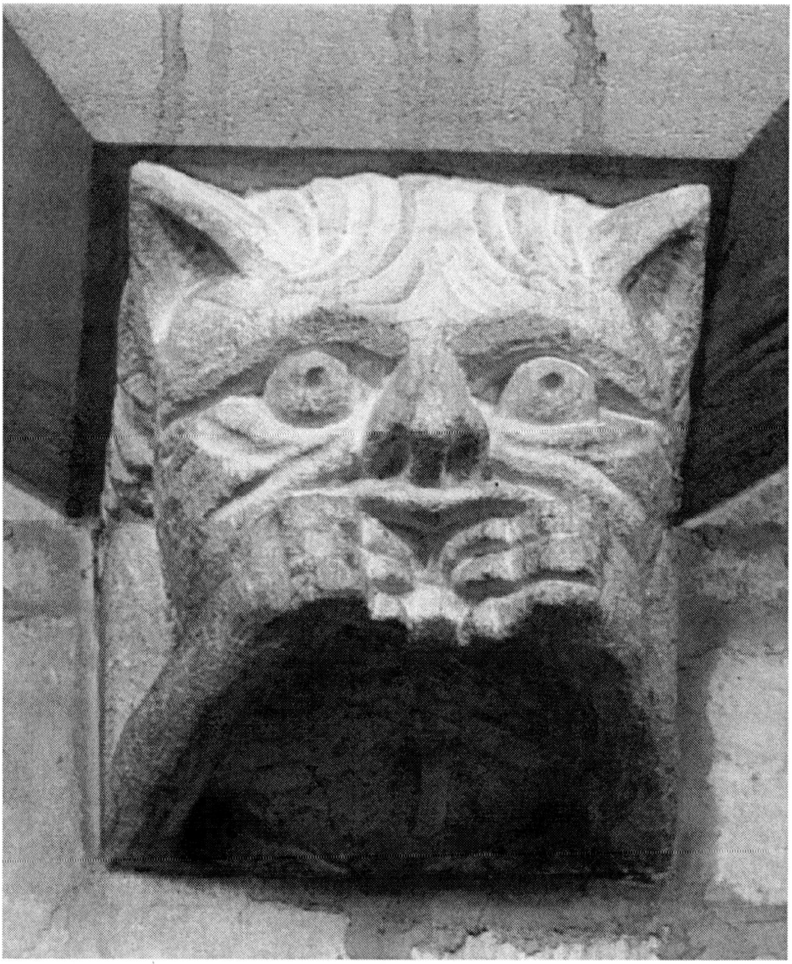

Gurning corbel, Sproxton.

as female exhibitionists, who evoke images of their fecundity by using their hands in a similar way to prominently display another part of their anatomy. There are no typical examples of sheela-na-gigs in Leicestershire or Rutland, although gargoyles at Illston and Stathern are somewhat similar.

There is a difference of opinion about whether the word should be spelt 'gurning' or 'girning'. Cumbrian dialect seems to favour the former, but Low Scots and northern Irish dialects use the latter form, although with the meaning 'turning down the mouth to whinge or weep' (Anthony Weir, personal communication). The origins of the word appear to be shared with the word 'grin', which in turn comes from the Old English *grennian.*

Tongue pokers

Tongue pokers are clearly rather rude. But did their carvers see them as 'watered down' versions of something much ruder? It would be too much to expect the survival in a church of any carving whose masculinity was too obvious —although there is a clearly male exhibitionist in Queniborough church roof. But, just as the gurning faces may be a polite version of female exhibitionists, so tongue-poking faces have been seen as the counterpart for the male. (The first to make this suggestion seems to be the otherwise staid M.D. Anderson, 1971.)

Another explanation may be that it is world-wide gesture of defiance. The Maoris have taken this almost to an art-form with the

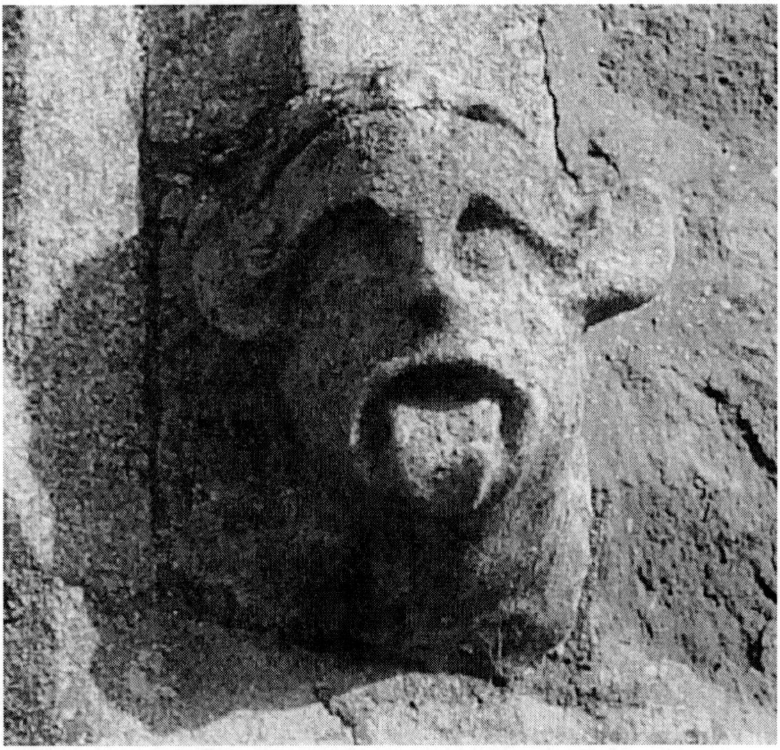

Tongue poker, Belton in Rutland.

ceremonial war dances which feature aggressive displays of tongue poking. In the city of Basel, Switzerland, a tongue-poking face known as the Laellenkoenig (literally 'lolling king' —the tongue actually wags in and out) overlooks the Rheinbrucke (the main bridge over the River Rhine). This insulting gesture seems to reflect long-standing bad feelings between the residents of the main part of Basel and 'Little Basel' across the river.

One of the four faces on the Romanesque font at Greetham has a descending tongue whose length is as great as the face. Most examples of tongue-pokers have less extreme anatomical distortions.

Belvoir Angels

So-called 'Belvoir angels' are a distinctive decoration on late eighteenth and early nineteenth century tombstones, typically those made from Swithland slate. They are more common in the north of Leicestershire and take their name from the Vale of Belvoir — although they are not especially common in the churchyards in the Vale itself. They usually take the form of a face between a pair of wings.

Strictly they are not angels at all. To the people who carved them, they depicted the soul of the deceased ascending to heaven.

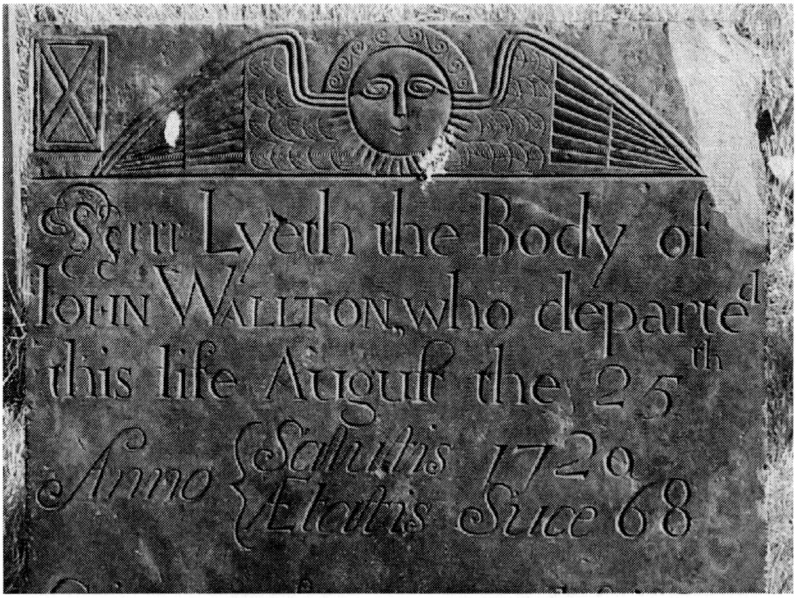

Belvoir angel, Burton Lazars.

Gazetteer

Allexton

Two lions with rather human faces grace either side of the south porch of St Peter's church (Landranger Ref. 141:817004). These are probably fifteenth or early sixteenth century.

The church dates to about 1160. The chancel arch capitals and the tower arcade (with a tiny head abutting the tower) are Romanesque.

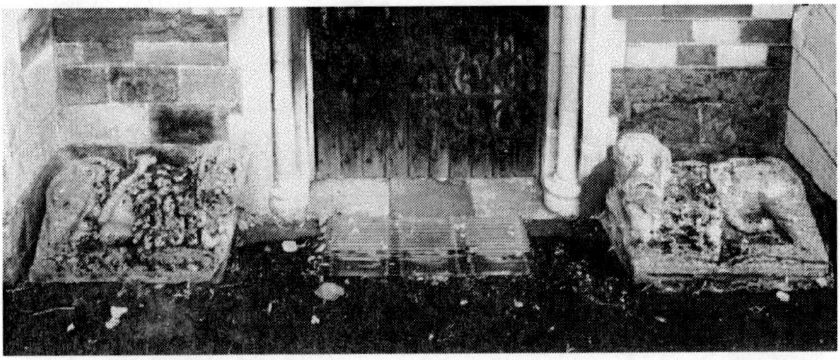

Carved lions guarding the porch of St Peter's church, Allexton.

Appleby Magna

In the kitchen of a fourteenth century moated farmhouse (Landranger Ref. 128:316098) are various unsophisticated carvings, including a carving of St Michael with a dragon, and a panel of 'nonsense' writing, probably intended to ward off evil (see photographs overleaf). These carvings were possibly removed from the church, maybe when it was rebuilt in the early fourteenth century. More probably, the carvings may be sixteenth century or later, done in a deliberately 'archaic manner'.

Asfordby

All Saints church (Landranger Ref. 129:708189) is mostly fourteenth and fifteenth century, although there are some fragments of Romanesque masonry. The wooden roof of the nave is fifteenth century; one of the roof bosses depicts a fine green man and twelve wooden angels support the roof while playing musical instruments. Under the angels there are interesting stone corbel heads, including a gurning man. In the south transept is a very small face that is also

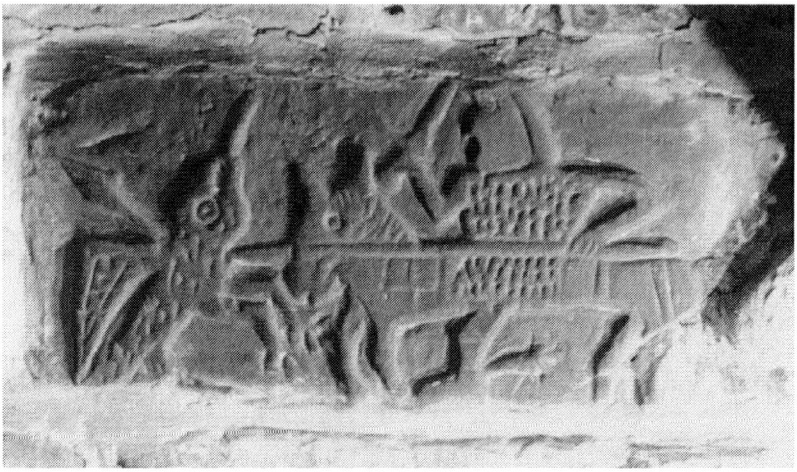

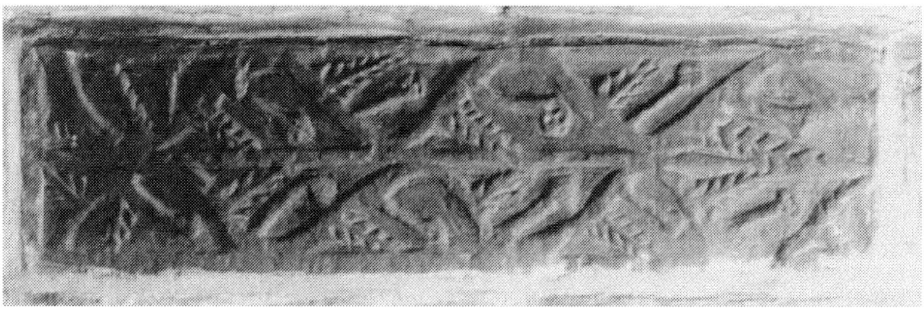

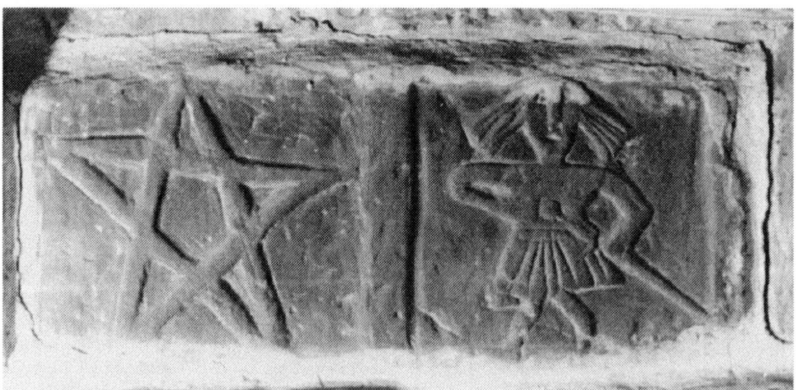

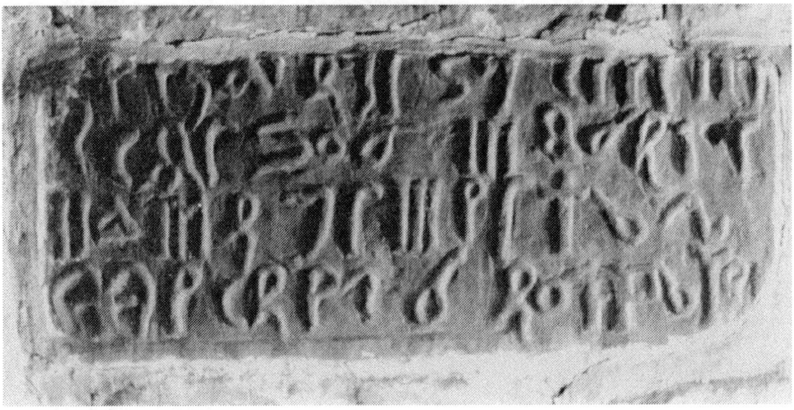

Opposite and above: *The carvings inside the moated farmhouse at Appleby Magna. Photographs by Bob Jarrett.*

Below: The gatehouse to the fourteenth century moated farmhouse.

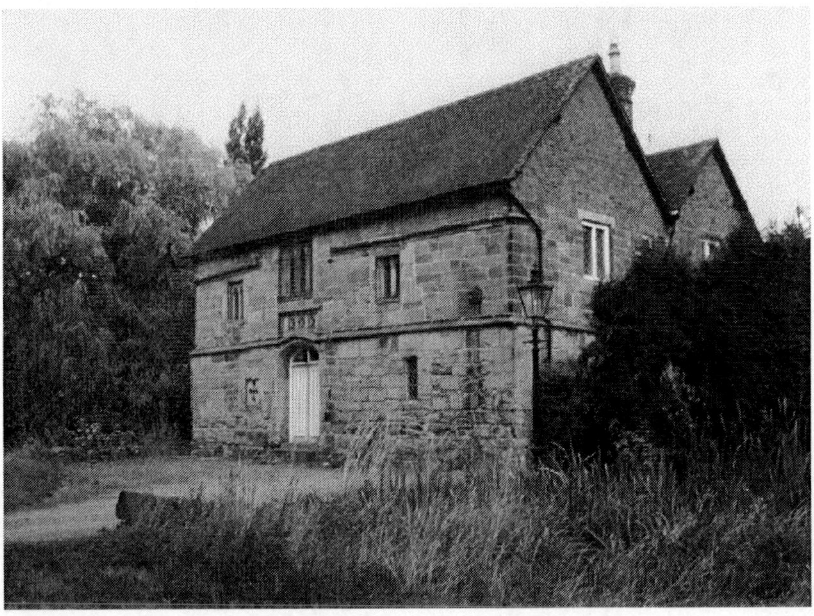

gurning. Around the church there is ballflower decoration —but, on closer inspection, some of the ballflowers turn out to be heads.

Three fragments from the shaft of an Anglo-Saxon cross now stand in the church (see photograph on page 3). One of these fragments shows a dragon, another a bishop with a crosier. These carvings are usually dated to between the ninth and eleventh centuries.

In addition there is a medieval preaching cross by the main road (Landranger Ref. 129:708190). The shaft of this was replaced in about 1920 after an early motoring accident demolished the original.

Ashby Folville

In the nave of St Mary's church (Landranger Ref 129:706120) are some of the most splendid carvings in the county. A set of stone corbels that probably date from about 1220 support painted wooden musical angels of about 1520. There are also wooden roof bosses of about 1520 with various decorations including foliate heads. All the wooden carvings are believed to be still painted in their original colours.

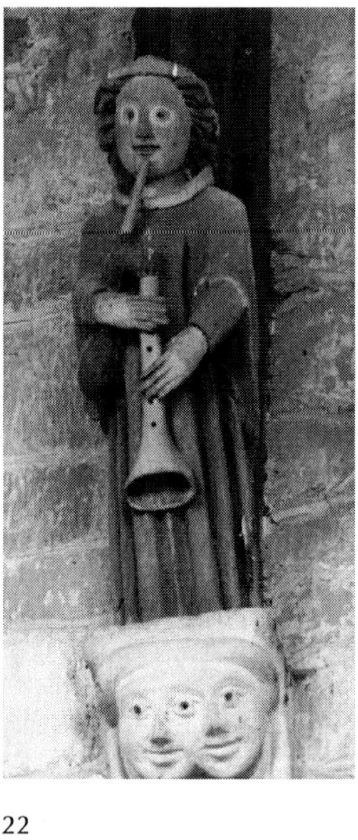

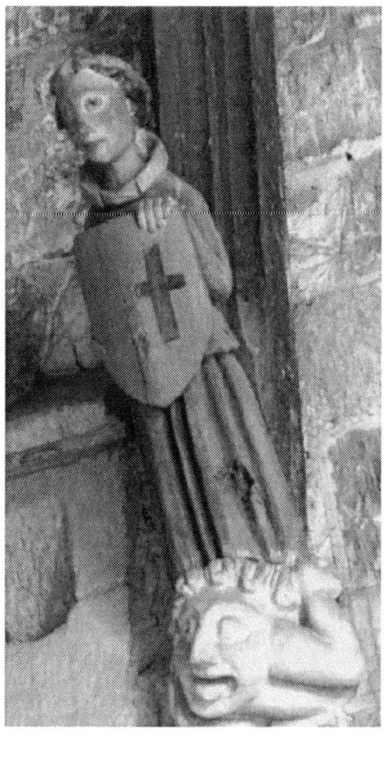

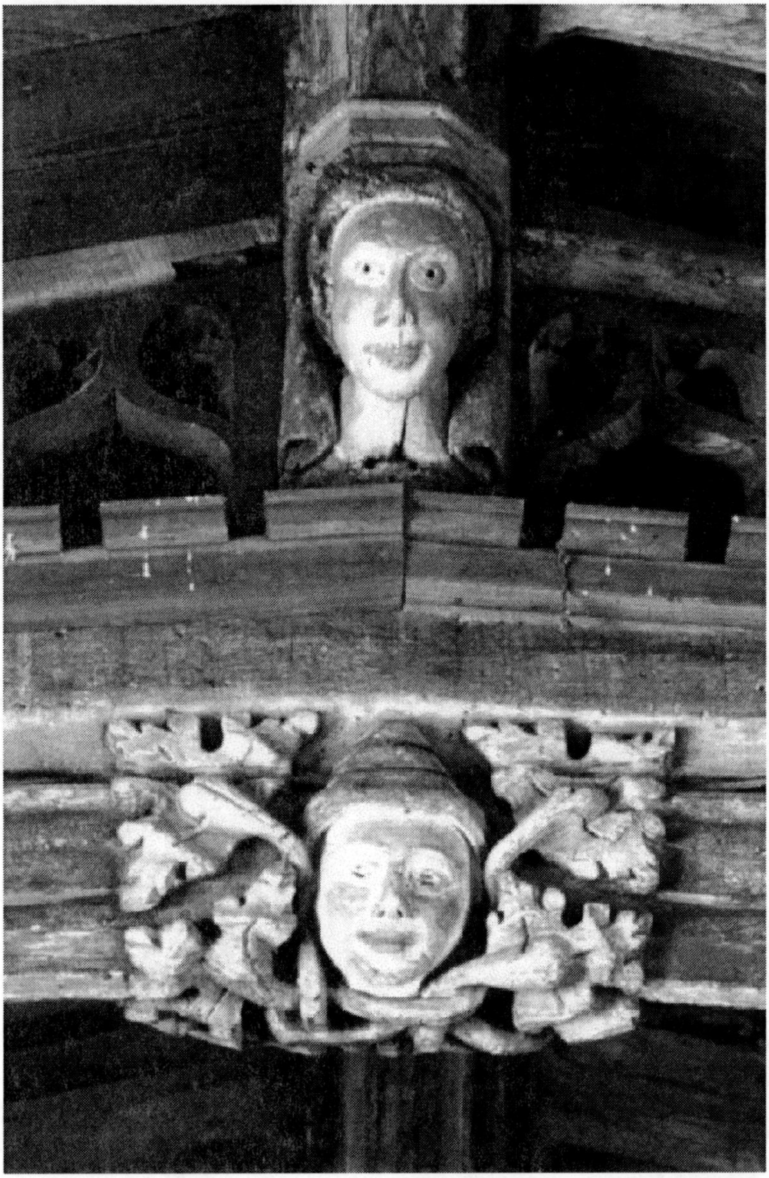

Above: *One of four roof bosses of about 1520 in the nave of Ashby Folville church. These have retained their original paint.*

Opposite: *Painted wooden angels of about 1520, on stone corbels of about 1220; Ashby Folville.*

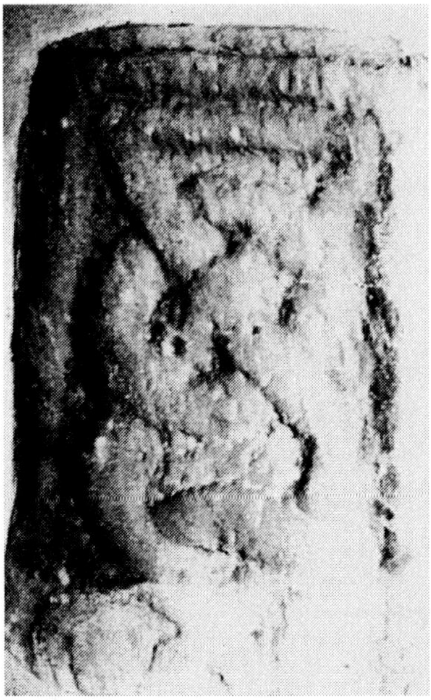

Left: *Anglo-Saxon cross shaft fragment, Aston Flamville.*

In the north-east of the nave by the chancel arch is a gurning head. On the south wall of the nave is a horned head and a double-head with three eyes.

The Romanesque font has architectural arcades and three small animal heads.

In the side chapel are several well-restored sepulchral effigies that are among the best in the county.

There is also a stone mensa (pre-Reformation stone altar) in the south aisle. This would have formed the top of the altar until the sixteenth or seventeenth centuries.

Aston Flamville

In St Peter's church (Landranger Ref 140:463927) a fragment of Anglo-Saxon interlace carving is set in the north-west nave wall. There is one Romanesque window and the chancel is thirteenth century. There is a kneeling effigy and an incised tomb. The rest of the church dates to 1873–4, except the lychgate which was constructed in 2000.

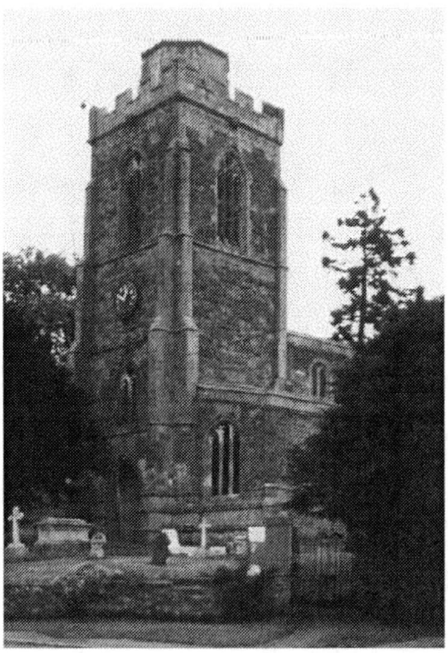

Beeby

All Saints church (Landranger Ref. 141:664083) dates to the thirteenth century, although only the south doorway survives from this time. The tower is fourteenth century, as is the screen inside.

The incomplete spire, known as Beeby tub, is attributed to a quarrel between two brothers. These were the masons who had

Left: *Beeby church and 'tub'.*

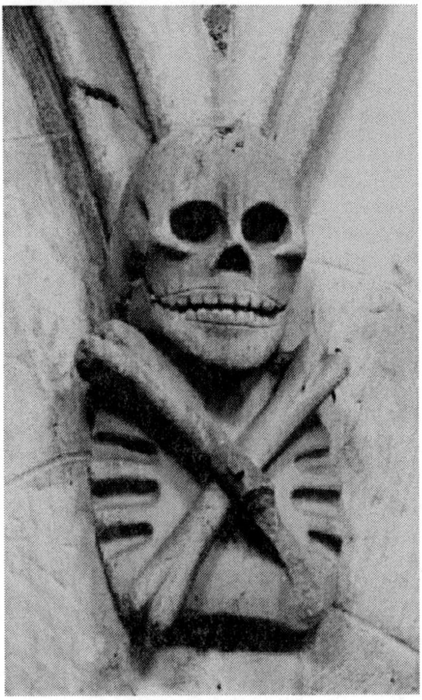
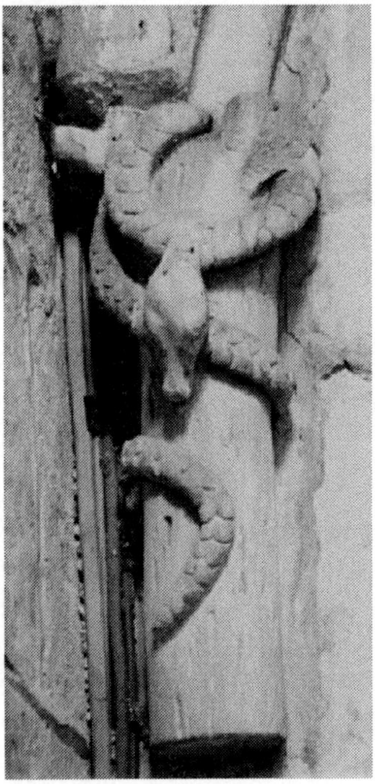

Unusual carvings on the arch springers in Beeby church.

completed the needle-like spire at Queniborough. But at Beeby they argued over costs and the ability of the tower to take the weight of the steeple. One day the argument led to a scuffle, and the two both slipped from the tower to their deaths. As a local rhyme recounts:

> Beeby Tub was to have been a spire.
> Two brothers fought and broke their backs,
> And so 'twas built no higher.

The chancel is nineteenth century. The fascinating carvings in the arch springers of the nave are possibly of the same date.

Belton in Rutland
St Peter's church (Landranger Ref. 141:816014) stands on a mound. The building retains evidence of a fire in the thirteenth century. The font is also thirteenth century. On the drain of the piscina in the south aisle is a monster's head. On the south side of the exterior there are many gargoyles, including one gurning. One window on the south

aisle is decorated by a tongue-poker with pronounced ears. A double partial effigy and medieval tomb covers can be found on top of the churchyard wall.

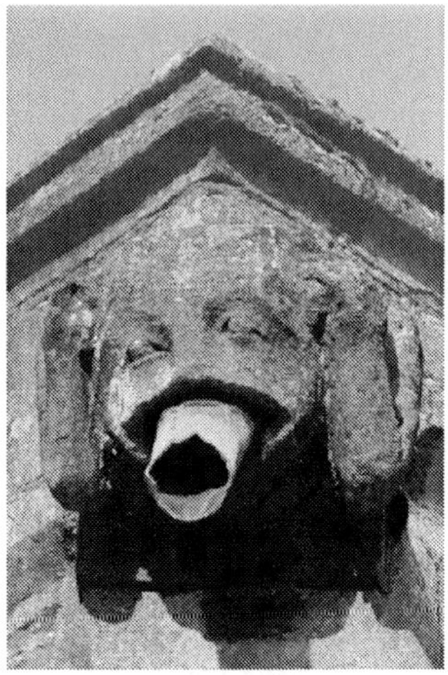

Medieval carvings on Belton in Rutland church. (See also photograph on page 17.)

Bottesford

The impressive church of St Mary the Virgin (Landranger Ref. 130:807392) is the biggest village church in Leicestershire, with the highest spire in the county at 210 feet (approx. 68 metres).

On the outside are a variety of heads and some impressive gargoyles. On the south aisle is a gargoyle of a bell-ringer (although it is not unique, as often claimed, as there is another example of a bell-ringing gargoyle not that far away at Branston).

Inside, the panels of the font alternate flowers and figures that anticipate the 'Belvoir Angels' found on the eighteenth and nineteenth century Swithland slate tombstones. The font base has eight heads, all tongue-poking.

In the north aisle of the arch to the side chapel there is a head with a serpent-like worm coming out of its mouth. Between each of the windows in the clerestory are various heads including two tongue-pokers, one of which has rather pointed ears —the initial impression is of a Romanesque beaked head.

On the nave arcade the arch springers have very three-dimensional animals including a monkey's head, two lions, a winged dragon, a non-winged dragon, and, at the south-east end, an upside-down man. In the same corner of the nave, on the chancel arch wall, is a head with a single, central eye.

All these carvings inside are difficult to date, although I suspect most are probably of the sixteenth century.

In addition, Bottesford church has been called 'the Westminster Abbey of Leicestershire' as it contains many splendid sepulchral

Opposite page: *Bottesford carvings.*
Top left: *Falling man on nave arcade. (See also photo on page 12.)*
Top right: *One-eyed grotesque, chancel arch wall.*
Right: *Gargoyle depicting a bell-ringer on outside of south aisle.*

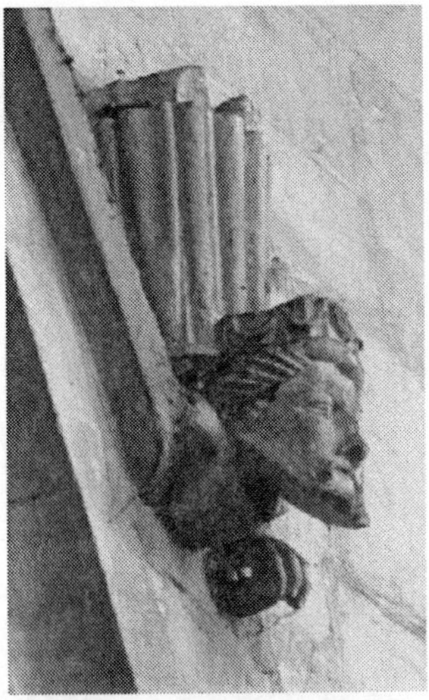

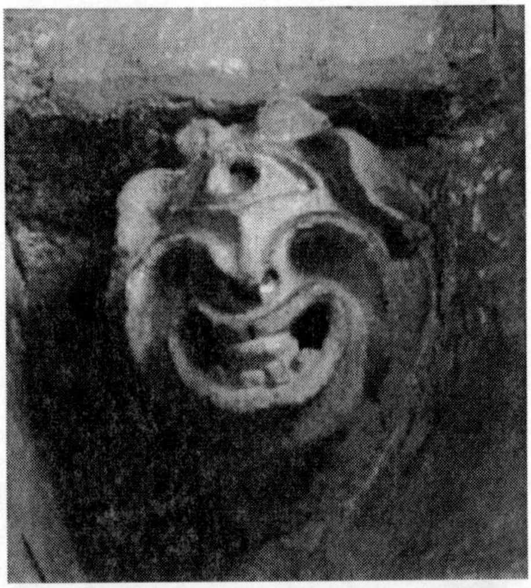

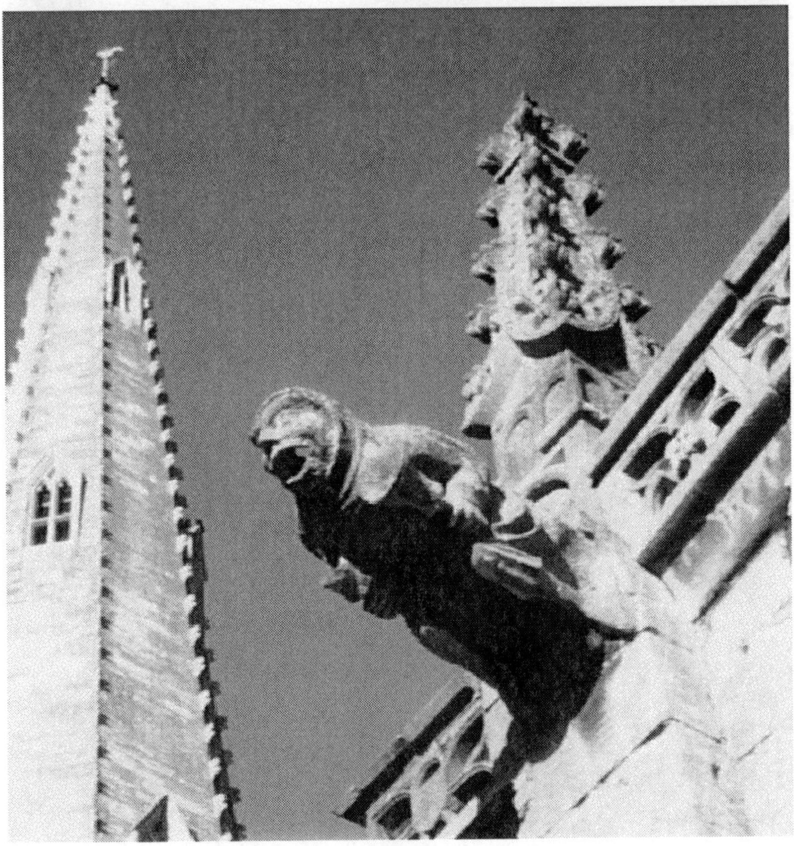

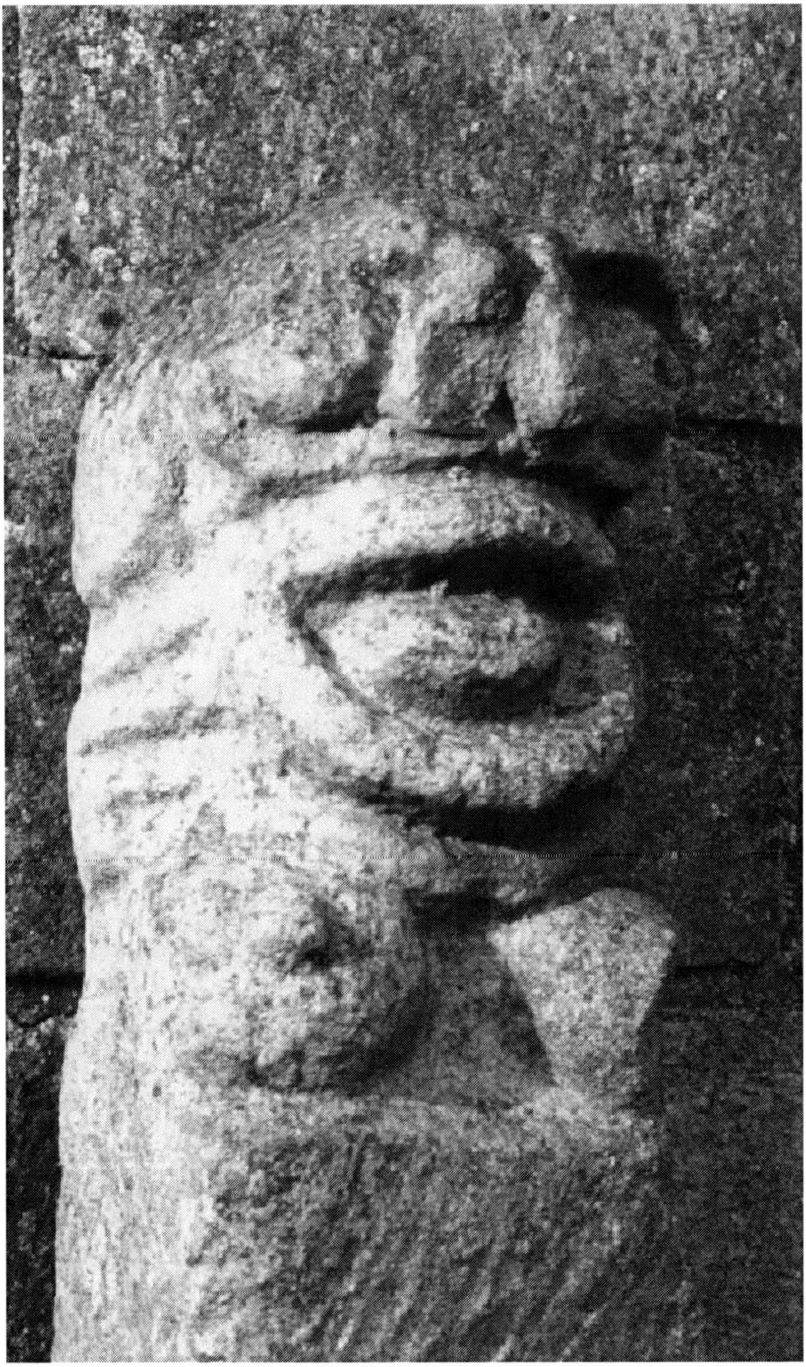

effigies, indeed the entire chancel is dominated by these marble or alabaster displays of self-importance. Many commemorate the Manners family, Lords of Rutland for eight hundred years.

Braunston in Rutland

All Saints church (Landranger Ref. 141:833066) has a striking but enigmatic carving that stands in the churchyard on the west side of the church close to the tower. It was used (face down) as the doorstep for the church for many years. Since its rediscovery early in the twentieth century it has been a source of mystery and amazement. The figure is often referred to as the 'Earth Mother' or a Goddess, implying pre-Christian origins. One scholar has stated, without any convincing reasons, that she is Iron Age in date. Others place her in the Anglo-Saxon period. But there are no known carvings of such antiquity remotely similar in appearance. Saxon and Norman iconographers say 'She's not one of ours', and the medieval specialists also shrug and mutter without shedding any light on her date or counterparts.

The large block of uncarved stone suggests that the figure was carved to jut out from a wall. In Somerset such carvings, known as 'hunky punks', decorate the towers of some churches and are dated to the fourteenth century. If the Braunston figure was originally on the tower it may have been removed during the eighteenth century restoration of the tower and been reused as the doorstep. There is no strong reason to suppose that the figure is older than the thirteenth or fourteenth century. The same research that shows that Green Men are *not*, as has come to be widely believed in recent years, some cryptic survivals of pre-Christian religion also discounts the possibility that this Braunston figurine was originally intended to depict a pagan goddess. However she most certainly has been reinvented as a pagan image in the last twenty or thirty years.

Braunston church also has a Romanesque doorway, chancel arch and font. There are traces of medieval wall paintings. Look out too for the tiny (about 3 inches high) heads in the north aisle. In the churchyard two slate tombstones (dated 1787 and 1795) depict the Resurrection.

Breedon on the Hill

Breedon on the Hill translates as 'hill hill on the hill'! 'Bre' is the Celtic word for hill and 'don' the Old English counterpart. Clearly

Opposite: *The enigmatic female carving outside Braunston church.*

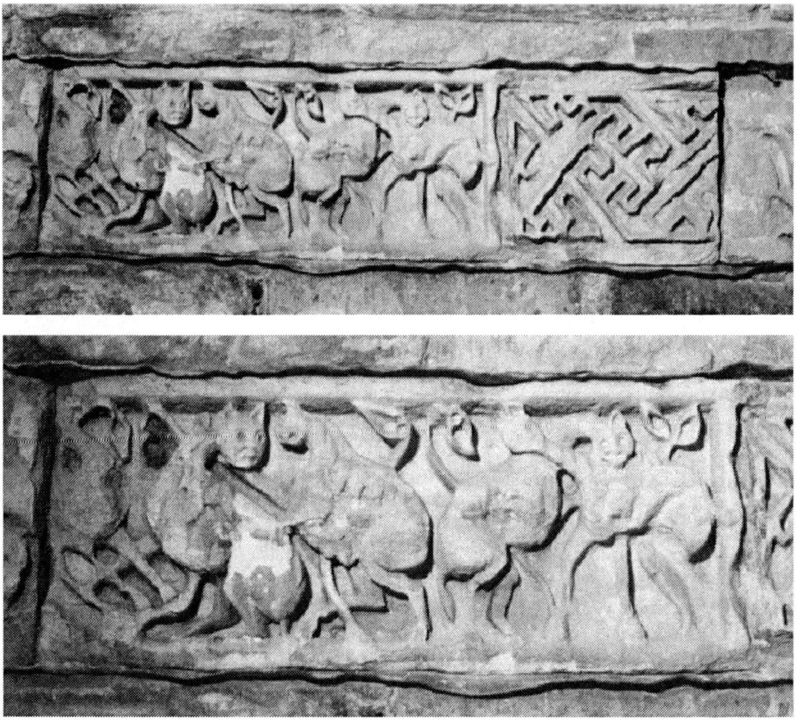

Two of the superb eighth century Anglo-Saxon friezes in Breedon church.

over the years the meaning of earlier languages was lost. The hill is indeed a prominent landmark, more so before twentieth century quarrying removed over half of it. The hill is comprised of Carboniferous limestone, extracted for use as roadstone.

The summit of the hill was surrounded by the earthworks of an Iron Age hill fort, now mostly quarried away. Inside this is the church of St Mary and St Hardolph (who is assumed to be the founder). The present building (Landranger Ref. 129:405234) is just a small part of the medieval buildings. Before these there had been at least two Anglo-Saxon churches. The first one was a minster church founded about 675.

From the seventh to ninth centuries the monastery at Breedon flourished, even providing an Archbishop of Canterbury, but was destroyed by the Danes in the mid-ninth century. It was re-endowed with land in 1120 and developed as a small Augustinian abbey,

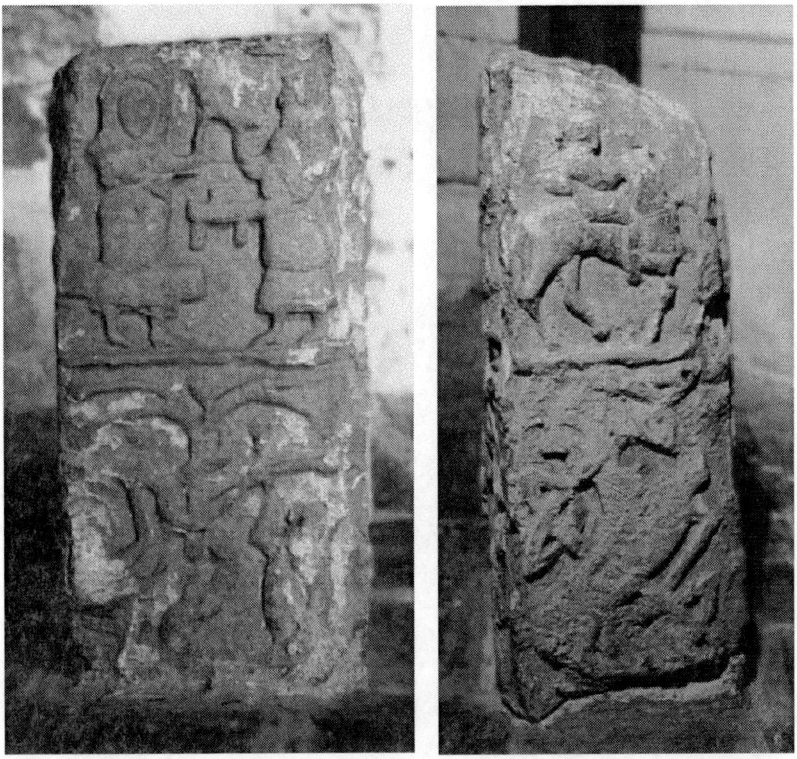

Two of the Anglo-Scandinavian cross shaft fragments in Breedon church.

dependent on Nostell (Yorkshire). The present building is a small part of the abbey church —what is now the western tower was originally a central tower.

Breedon church contains a wealth of Anglo-Saxon carvings of national importance. Most date from the eighth century (i.e. the *second* Anglo-Saxon building here). The friezes are unequalled in quantity, quality and preservation. Some have deeply incised interlace patterns, other have animated animals among vine-like foliage. Most of the vines are 'inhabited' with highly stylised mythical beasts. The skill of carving so deeply such small details is itself impressive; even more astounding is that the animals should appear so animated as they prance and frolic their way across the various scenes.

During the eighth century the Mercian kingdom, under King Offa, was at its most powerful and had developed contacts with the

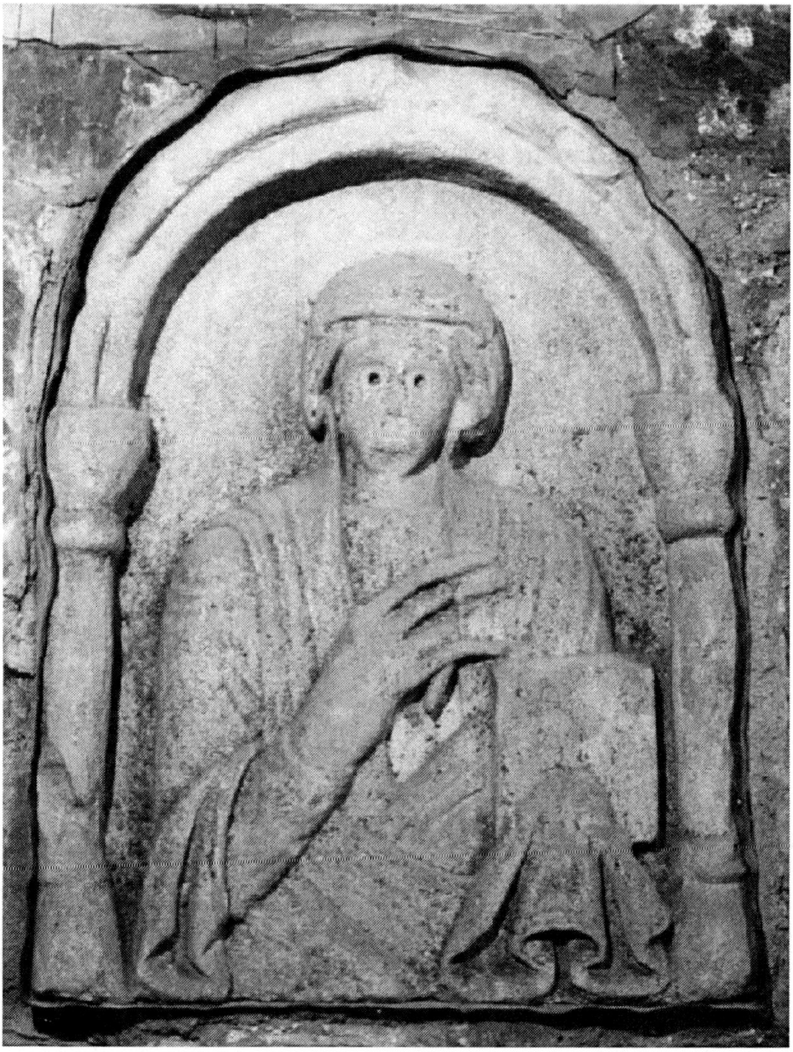

An apostle or saint carved in the eighth or ninth century, Breedon church.

Holy Roman Empire and Charlemagne. The exchange of illuminated books, needlework, and jewellery led to dramatic changes in artistic style. The Breedon carvings show influences from Northumbrian, Irish and Byzantine art, as well as individual designs that may be in a local Mercian tradition.

The Breedon artists were strongly influenced by Coptic art from Egypt, which fits in well with assumptions about the strong connections established by the Roman Church between the Middle East and all parts of Europe.

These sculptures are stylistically close to the Lindisfarne Gospels and St Chad's Gospels (from Lichfield), and other examples now in Rome, Paris and Stockholm. More locally, the porch of Bakewell church (Derbyshire) has a collection of fragments of Anglo-Saxon carving of a similar date.

Like these illuminated Gospels, the sculptures were originally coloured and the friezes would probably have formed a continuous decorative band around the outside.

In the south aisle are most of the carvings of individual human figures whose identity is now doubtful (but are probably apostles or other saints).

In the north of the nave are fragments of the cross shafts in Anglo-Viking or Anglo-Scandinavian style of the ninth century. One of these has two panels, which have been interpreted as the Biblical story of Adam and Eve and the other as a pagan scene of the entry into Valhalla (although there are alternative interpretations).

One of the carvings inaccessible to most visitors is in the belfry (kept locked) and depicts a winged angel holding a crook in one hand and giving a Byzantine-style blessing with the other; this is dated to about 1000 and is in the Winchester school style.

More information on the Anglo-Saxon carvings can be found in Bailey (1990), Clapham (1928) and Williams (no date).

Also in Breedon church are some splendidly carved effigies of the sixteenth century. These are monuments to the Shirley family and include a gruesome cadaver, to remind the onlooker of the ultimate fate of us all.

Brooke

The interior of St Peter's church (Landranger Ref. 141:850057) is quite remarkable as it has completely escaped the attention of Victorian restorations. Some of the building, including the square font with arcading and the south doorway, is Romanesque (although the arch of the south doorway has, at some time, been restored so that is pointed rather than rounded). The hinges on the north door are late twelfth century and resemble fish bones or menacing centipedes.

The tower is thirteenth century. Much of the rest was rebuilt in 1579, which is an unusual time for church restoration. The box pews

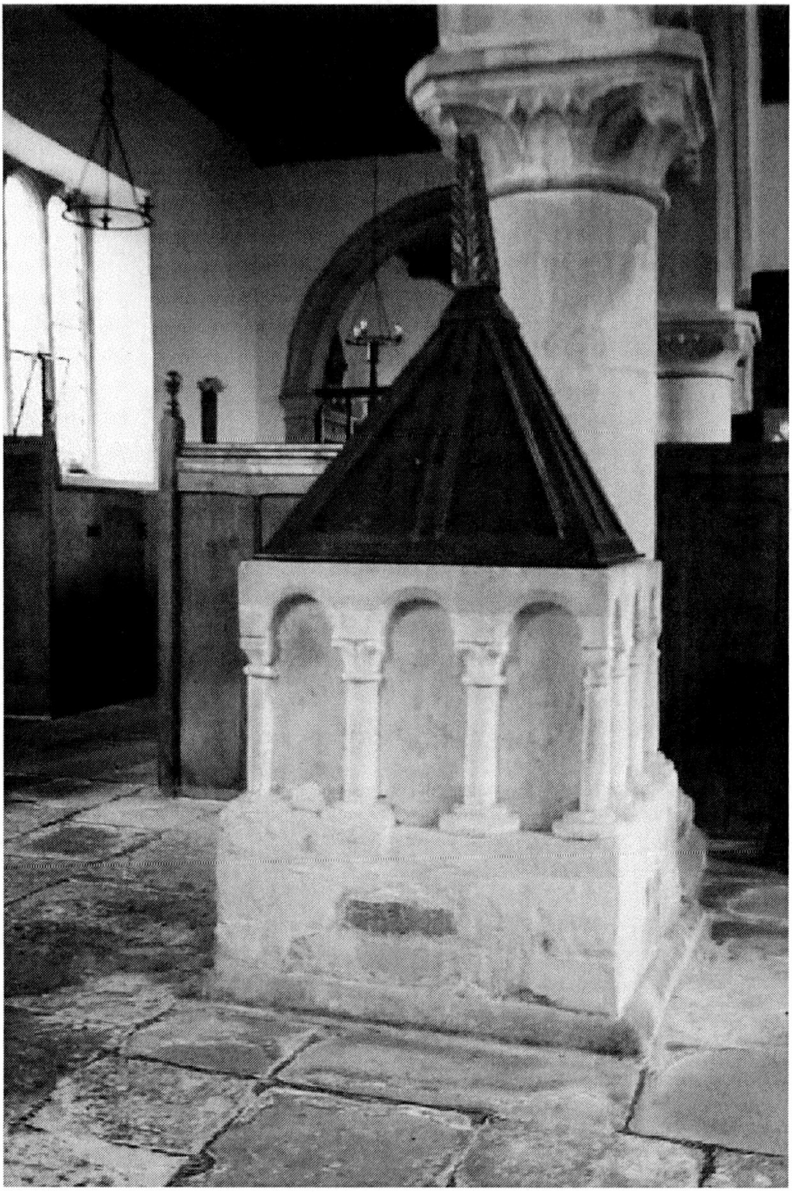

The Romanesque font in Brooke church.

and pulpit are also late sixteenth century. No other church in the country has remained as such a 'time capsule' from the late sixteenth century. There is a fine early seventeenth century effigy in the north aisle. Slightly later is the seventeenth century graffiti. Look out too for the parish chest made from a solid log.

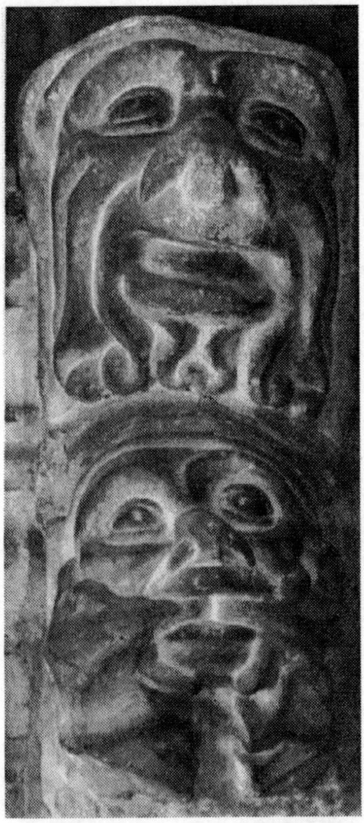

Unusual corbel with two faces. The lower one is a Green Man. Buckminster church.

Buckminster

St John the Baptist's church (Landranger Ref. 130:878231) is situated on exceptionally high ground; Hinckley church is intervisible.

The name Buckminster confirms that a seventh/eighth century Anglo-Saxon minster church was established there. The minsters at Buckminster and Breedon both stand on imposing hilltop sites.

The surviving building is mostly fourteenth and fifteenth century although the tower is late thirteenth century (with a fourteenth century spire), situated unusually at the east end of the aisle.

Inside there are forty medieval stone heads and eight faces on the fifteenth century font. Those in the north and south aisles are double, usually a man underneath a beast above. Of the ten figures in the nave, two are green men. These carvings demonstrate a good variety of styles and personalities, many quite lively.

Burton Overy

St Andrew's church (Landranger Ref. 141:677983) has a tower dating from about 1300. The remainder is mostly fifteenth century, including an oak screen and various corbel heads in the nave, plus a large head at waist height on an arch springer by the chancel arch. On the outside are gargoyles.

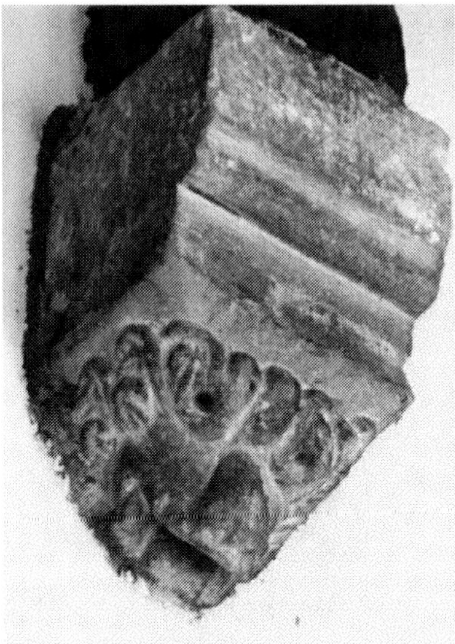

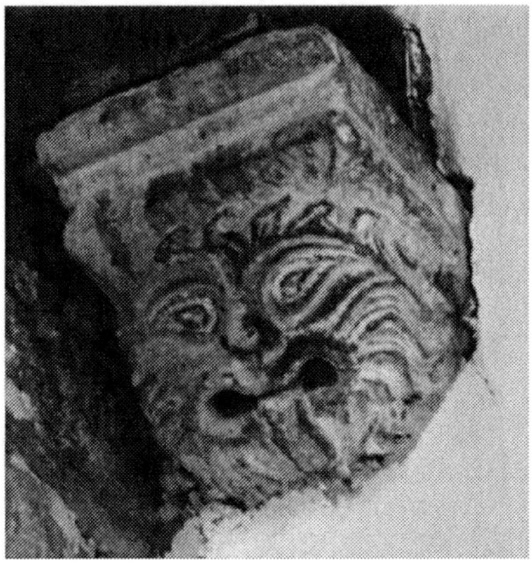

Two corbels in Burton Overy church.

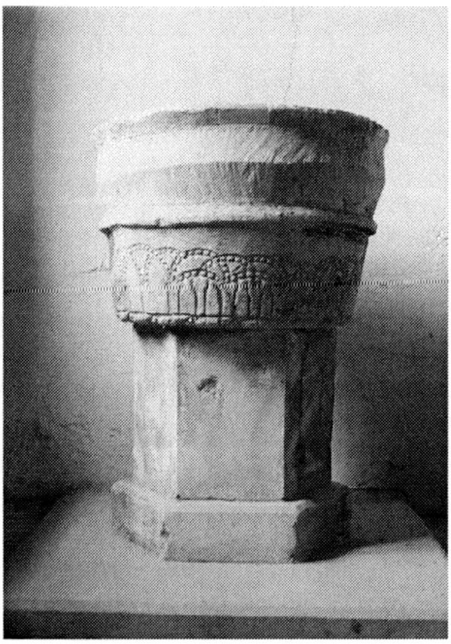

The Romanesque font in Chadwell church. Compare with the fonts at Foxton (photograph on page 5) and Brooke (photograph on page 34).

Chadwell
St Mary's church (Landranger Ref. 129:783246) is a gem. The building is entirely pre-1300. There is a blocked Romanesque arcade on the north side of the aisle and a Romanesque font decorated with wonderfully naive 'arcades'. The tower is thirteenth century.

Church Langton
St Peter's church (Landranger Ref. 141: 724934) is one of best churches in the county with a magnificent clerestoried interior. The chancel is fourteenth century and the tower fifteenth century.

A very interesting figure, probably Romanesque, is now rather hidden in the passage from the chancel to the vestry (see photograph on page 7). It depicts a naked figure wielding a Thor-

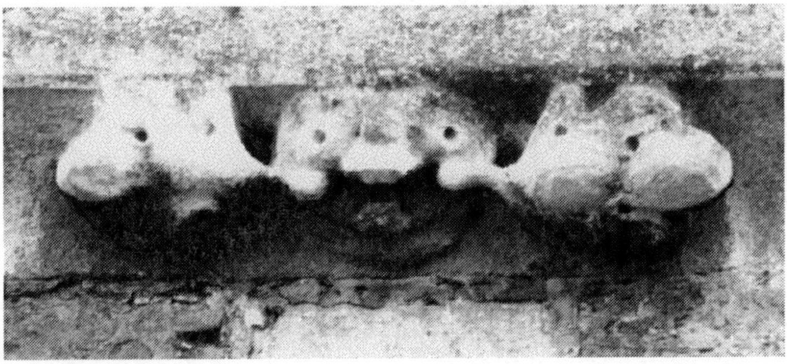

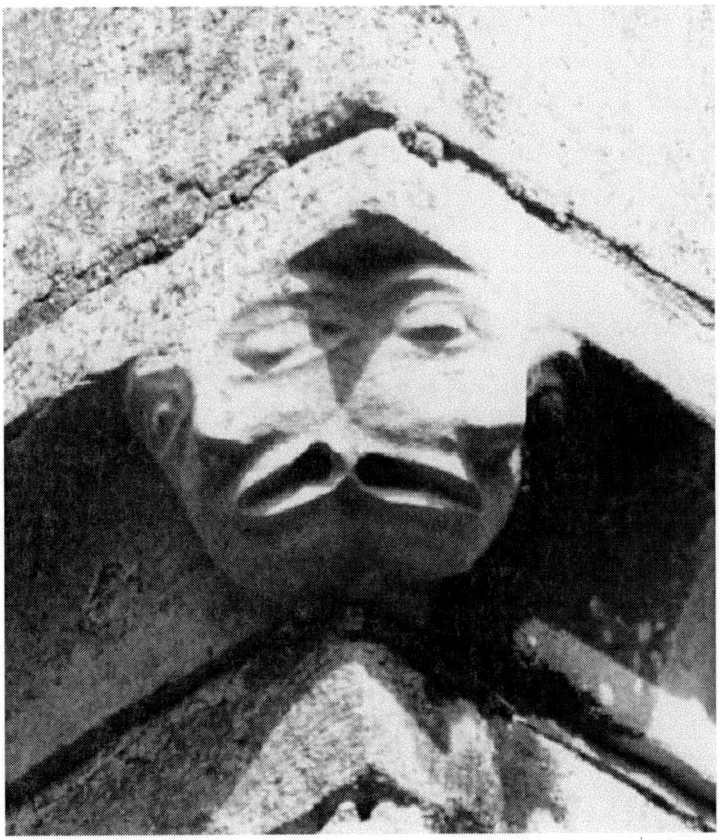

Two of the many fascinating carvings that form a frieze around St Peter's, Church Langton.

type hammer, or maybe a cross, in the right hand (the carving has been damaged in this area), and another shafted device, also damaged, in the other. The vitality of the pose contrasts with, say, the sedate cross-carrying clothed figure on, say, the Asfordby Anglo-Saxon cross fragment.

The exterior of this church has a feast of small heads forming the frieze around the north and south aisles. All are rather boss-eyed, some recognisably female in appearance. They include a double-handed gurning and two single-handed gurning, a tongue-poker and a green man (or is it a 'green monster'?). Perhaps the most notable motif on the south aisle frieze is on one corner where two faces intermingle. One of the gargoyles takes the form of a 'column swallower' (although, in this instance, he is a 'drainpipe swallower').

In the churchyard there are slate tombstones showing Adam and Eve with the Tree of Life and serpent; and Death directing a dart at Adam and the risen Christ below.

Cold Overton

St John the Baptist's church (Landranger Ref. 130:810102) is decorated with the most figurative carving that I have found so far in the counties. Every available architectural feature has been

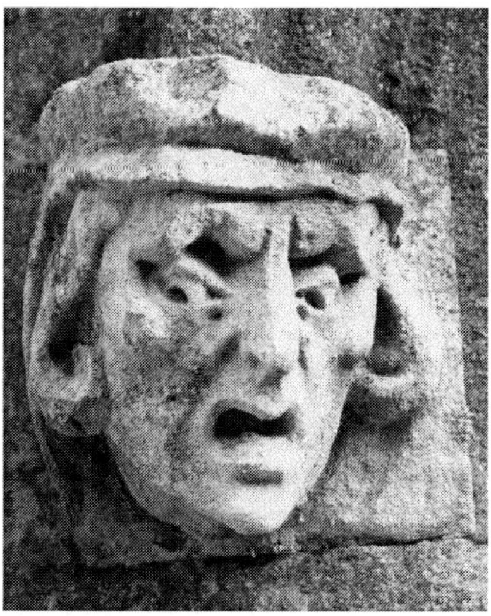

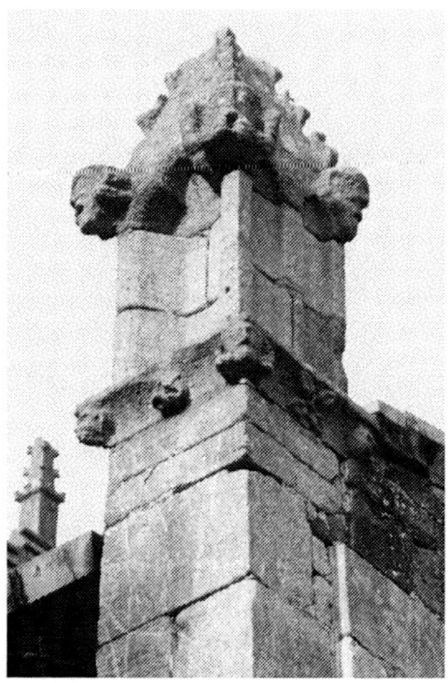

Left: *The most striking of the many faces on the exterior of Cold Overton church.*
Right: *One of the pinnacles with faces looking out from the corners.*

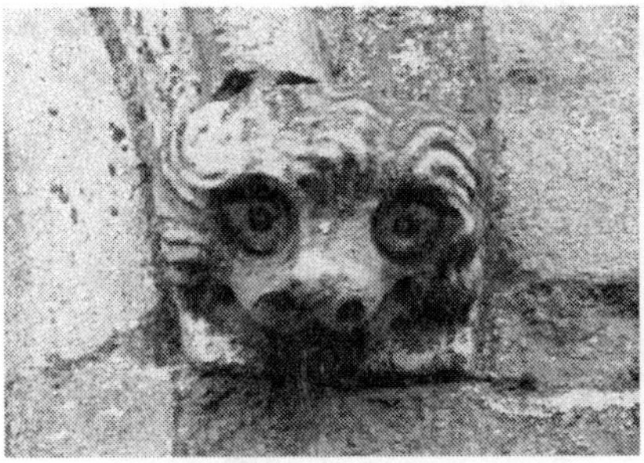

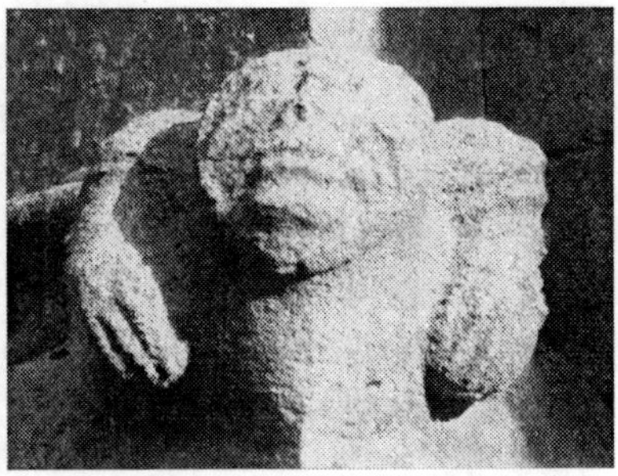

Two more of the very varied carvings on Cold Overton church.

ornamented to form a splendid display of the masons' skills. Numerous heads range in style from the most simple stylisations to highly animated caricatures.

Inside the porch are foliate heads, some in wood, others in stone. In the nave are fine corbel heads —one in the south-east corner is griffin-like, in the north-east is a beaked head. In the chancel is a blocked north door to the vestry which has two plain but clearly asymmetrical faces on the corbels; opposite is a sedilia with three similarly plain faces.

On the exterior north chancel wall are two unusual heads, one with hare-like ears, and the other stylised with two holes for eyes and what might be intended to be a beak.

Dating these heads is difficult; some may go back to the thirteenth and fourteenth century phases of building, but other appear to be seventeenth or maybe eighteenth century.

Additional splendours include the twelfth century stained glass in the south chancel window and remnants of fourteenth century wall paintings.

Just for fun, look out for the ironstone used to construct the porch which contains several well-preserved fossils of brachiopods (shellfish) and belemnites (slate-pencil shaped cuttlefish "bones").

Cranoe

The hilltop church of St Michael (Landranger Ref. 141:762953) has a thirteenth century tower but the rest was rebuilt in 1849. This presumably is the date of the curious label stops around the south door (see photograph on next page).

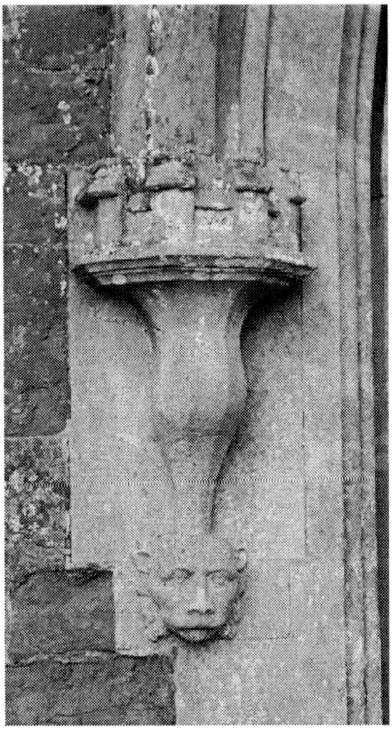

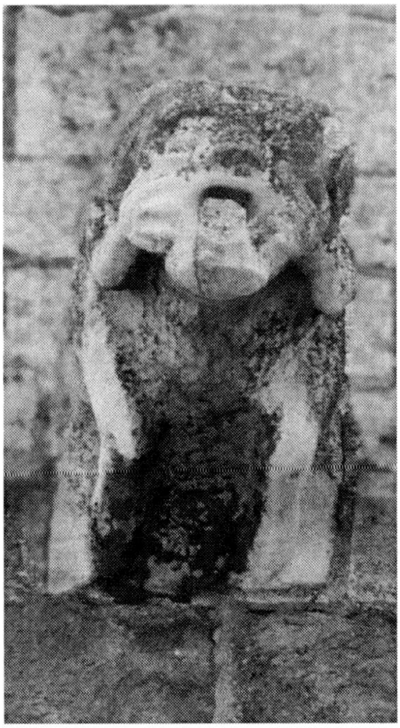

Top left: *Curiously carved label stop on the south door of Cranoe church.*
Top right and below: *Two views of the same gurning gargoyle on the tower of Eastwell church*

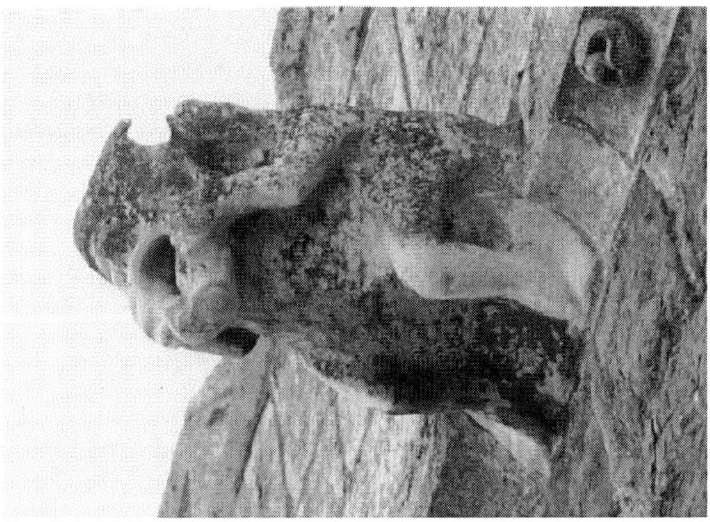

Eastwell

St Michael and All Angels church (Landranger Ref. 129:775285) is mostly thirteenth century. The fourteenth century stone chancel screen has survived, which is most unusual. This makes the interior of the church similar to the layout typical of pre-Reformation churches (and Eastern Orthodox churches up until the present day).

Over the inside of the south door porch is a green man. There are fragments of fourteenth century stained glass depicting a golden-haired angel. There are several gargoyles on the tower. One is gurning; one depicts a dragon or horse's head on its side.

Egleton

St Edmund's church (Landranger ref. 140:876075) is essentially a Romanesque church, although the aisles were removed in the thirteenth century. There is a Romanesque south doorway with a tympanum decorated with geometrical figures, a wyvern and what may be a lion. The chancel arch column shafts are either late Anglo-Saxon or early Romanesque. The original tower screen survives. The font is Romanesque, with wheel carvings. In the nave are a variety of small corbels.

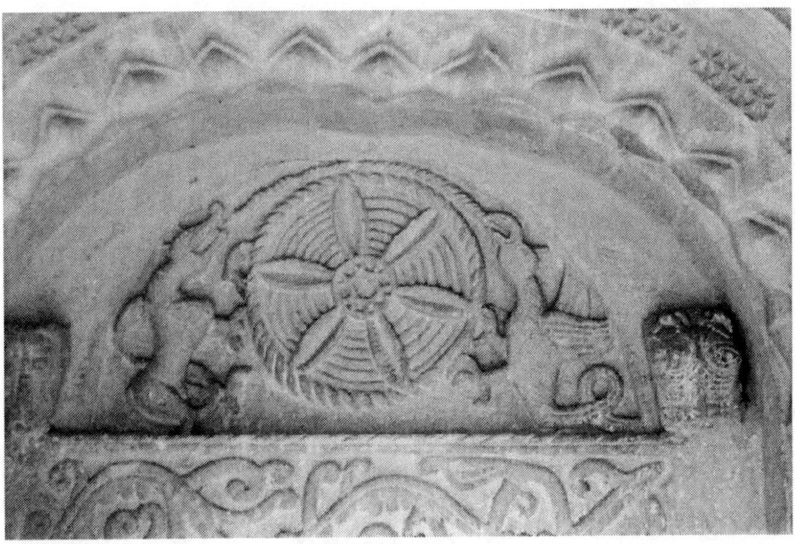

The tympanum at Egleton.

Essendine

On the south doorway of St Mary's church (Landranger Ref. 130: TF 049128) is one of the finest early Romanesque tympana in the area (see photograph on page 6) which depicts Christ in Majesty surrounded by a vesica and two angels. This design is more usual in France than in England. The door jambs are also carved, with figures that may be Adam and Eve under a tree; a stag under a tree; and two men with crooks; although unusual in England similar examples can be seen at Stoke Dry.

Foxton

St Andrew's church stands on a hilltop (Landranger Ref. 141: 699897). Inside there is a substantial fragment of an Anglo-Saxon cross shaft, decorated with interlace, and a fine Romanesque font (see photograph on page 5). The tower and chancel are late thirteenth century.

On the exterior of the north nave wall one of the window springers has a face with prominent ass-like (or maybe hare-like) ears, as does the left-hand springer of the north porch. The female counterpart on the porch has a square head-dress and a distinctly hag-like appearance with pointed chin and sunken features. The main entrance is through this porch, and the faces all look out over a steep slope towards the distant horizon of high east Leicestershire.

Gaddesby

The large and attractive church of St Luke (Landranger Ref. 129:690130) dates entirely from about 1260 to 1360. The spire is thirteenth century, the chancel fourteenth century. The south aisle is

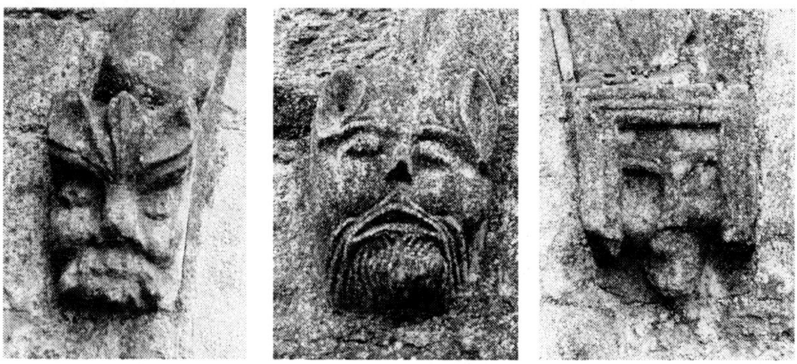

Three faces from Foxton. The human face in the middle has ass-like ears. The other two faces are on either side of the north door.

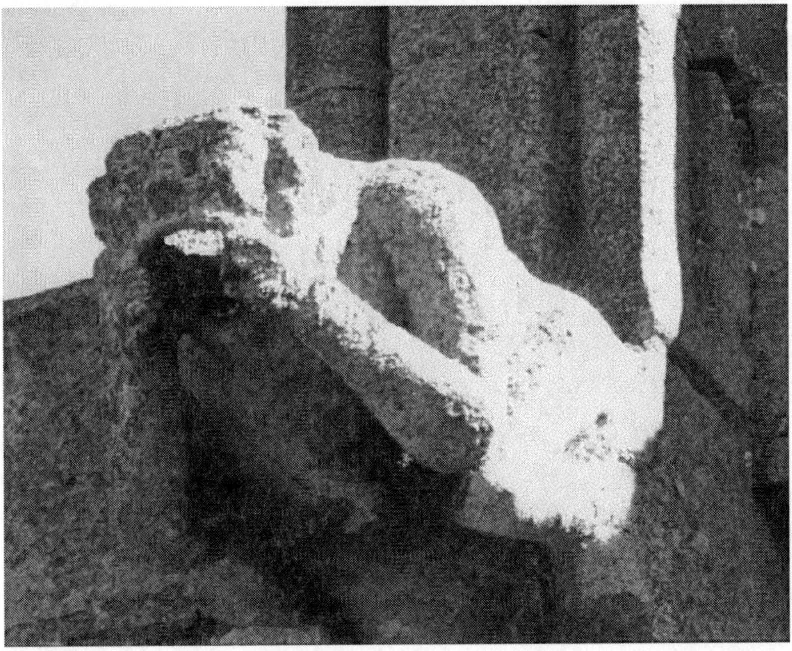

Gaddesby's gurning gargoyle.

a 'showpiece', reputedly created by the Knights Templars before their suppression in 1308. The exterior of the north aisle has heads and ballflower decoration dating from 1330 to 1350.

There is a large number of stone faces inside and out, mostly straight-forward male and female pairs probably of the late thirteenth century. Some of these faces are tongue-pokers. The most pronounced of these is on the exterior of the window at the west end of the south aisle; its counterpart is clearly horned. The gargoyles include a gurning face.

The interior is dominated by a near-life-size equestrian monument to Colonel Cheney, who had four horses shot under him at the battle of Waterloo and eventually died in 1848.

Greetham

St Mary's church (Landranger Ref. 130:92414) has a very fine Romanesque font with four carved heads: one bestial, two human and the fourth human but with a very elongated tongue. It is similar to the font at Hallaton.

In the south aisle west wall are other examples of Romanesque carving, including fragments of a tympanum. Also in the wall of the

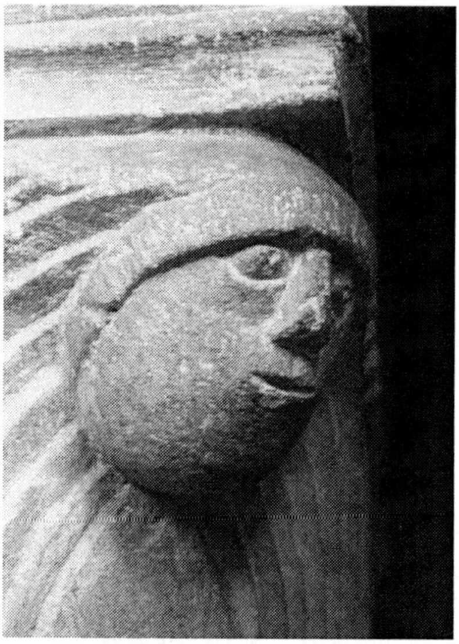

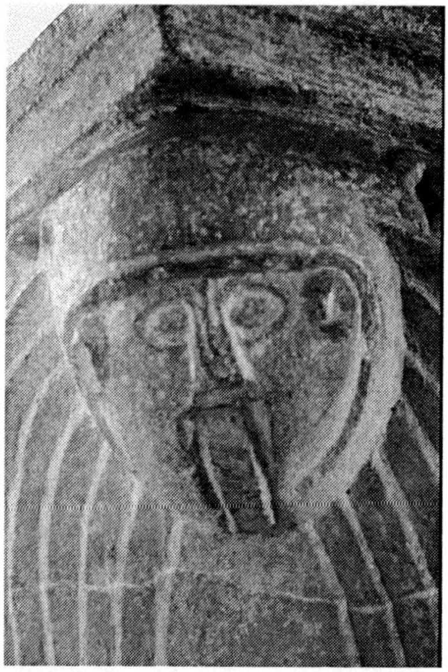

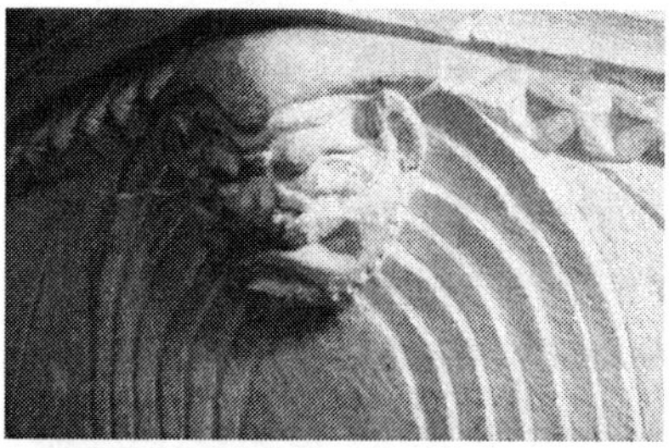

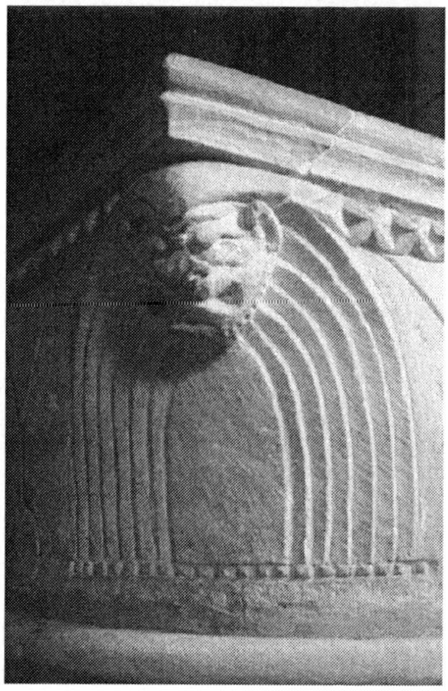

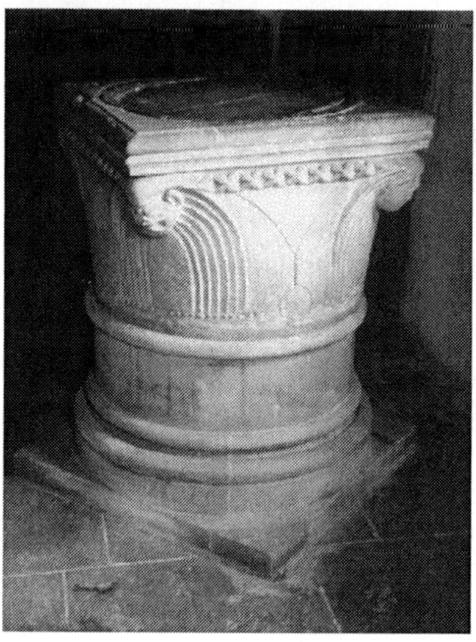

The superb Romanesque font at Greetham and the four faces, one a tongue-poker, carved on the corners.

south aisle are fragments of Anglo-Saxon masonry, one of which has fine interlace patterns and could be a cross shaft fragment.

Medieval carvings include several dozen small heads around the roof line of the nave and tower, some of which are distinctly demonic.

The workshop of Thomas Halliday (1816–84), one of the best stonemasons in Rutland, survives on the corner of Main Street and Great Lane (Landranger Ref. 130:926144). Into the walls are set fragments of tracery and other decorative stonework taken from churches he restored.

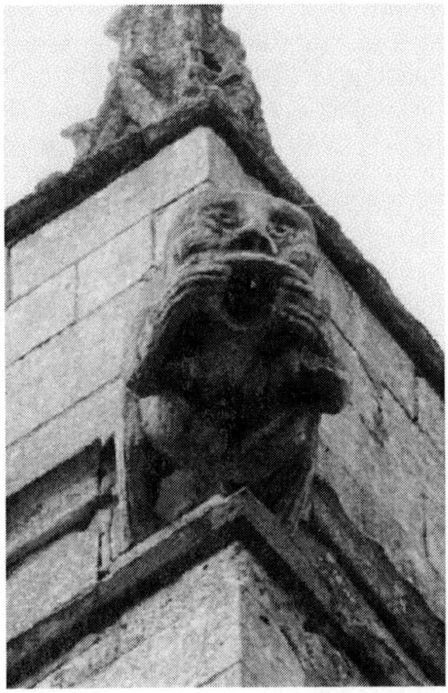

Above: *Grimston's gurning gargoyle.*
Below: *Thomas Halliday's workshop, Greetham.*

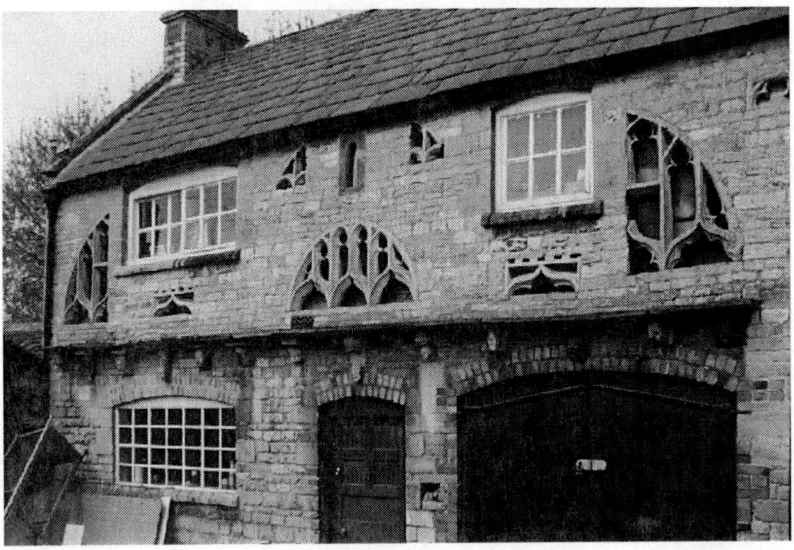

Grimston

St John the Evangelist church (Landranger Ref. 129:685219) is thirteenth century and stands on a pronounced mound amid a circular churchyard. There are four gargoyles on the tower. One is gurning (see photograph on previous page); another looks like a toothed fish or crocodile; the third is a figure bearing a shield and the fourth is too weathered to identify.

One of the wooden roof bosses in the nave is a face depicted with a crown and protruding tongue.

The churchyard contains the stump of a medieval cross and some interesting slate gravestones.

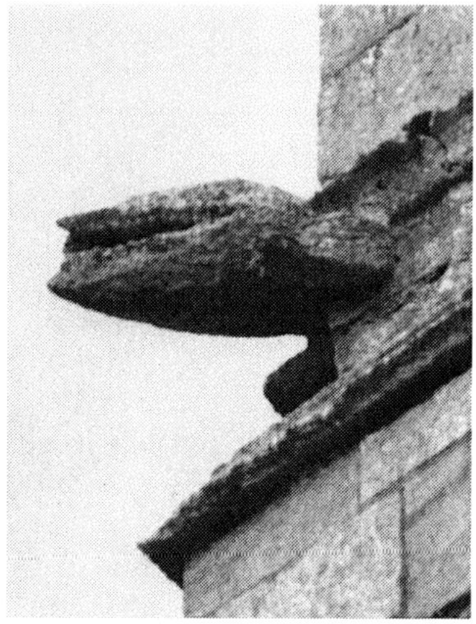

The 'crocodile' gargoyle on the tower of Grimston church.

Great Casterton

The church of St Peter and St Paul (Landranger Ref. 141:TF002088) is mostly thirteenth century, although there is a Romanesque font. It is reputedly built on the site of a Roman building (although not necessarily a temple, as is sometimes suggested).

Under an arch in the south wall is a thirteenth century effigy of a tonsured priest with remarkably large ears. In the north wall of the tower and the outside south wall are two other effigies of the same period.

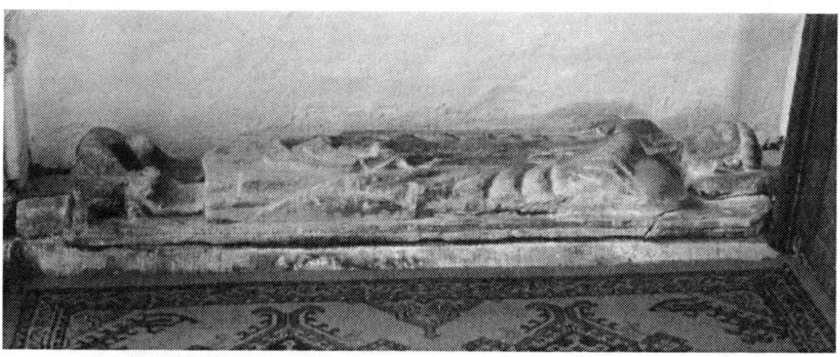

The effigy of a priest inside Great Casterton church.

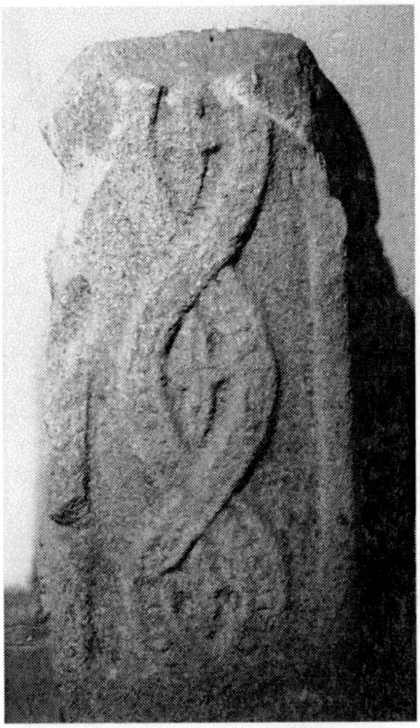

Great Easton Anglo-Saxon cross shaft fragment.

There is a tongue-poker in a springer of the arch of the south aisle. A gurning gargoyle can be seen on the south aisle.

In the churchyard is a slate tombstone with a rare depiction of the Resurrection; also another showing the sacrifice of Isaac.

Great Easton

St Andrew's church (Landranger Ref: 140:849933) includes Romanesque masonry. The tower is late thirteenth century. There are various heads on the arch springers and corbels. On the eastern-most pilaster of the north nave arcade there are two interesting heads. In the 1980s a fragment from an Anglo-Saxon cross shaft was discovered.

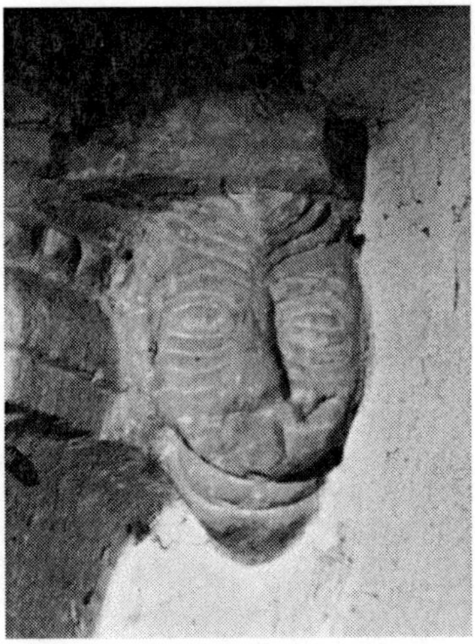

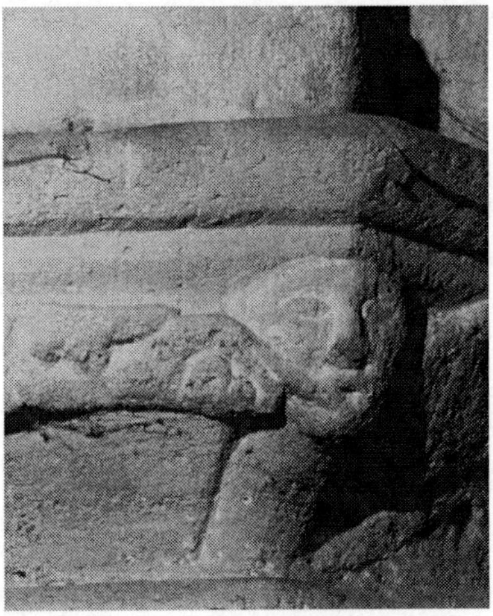

Two of the curious medieval carvings in Great Easton church. The one on the right is a green man.

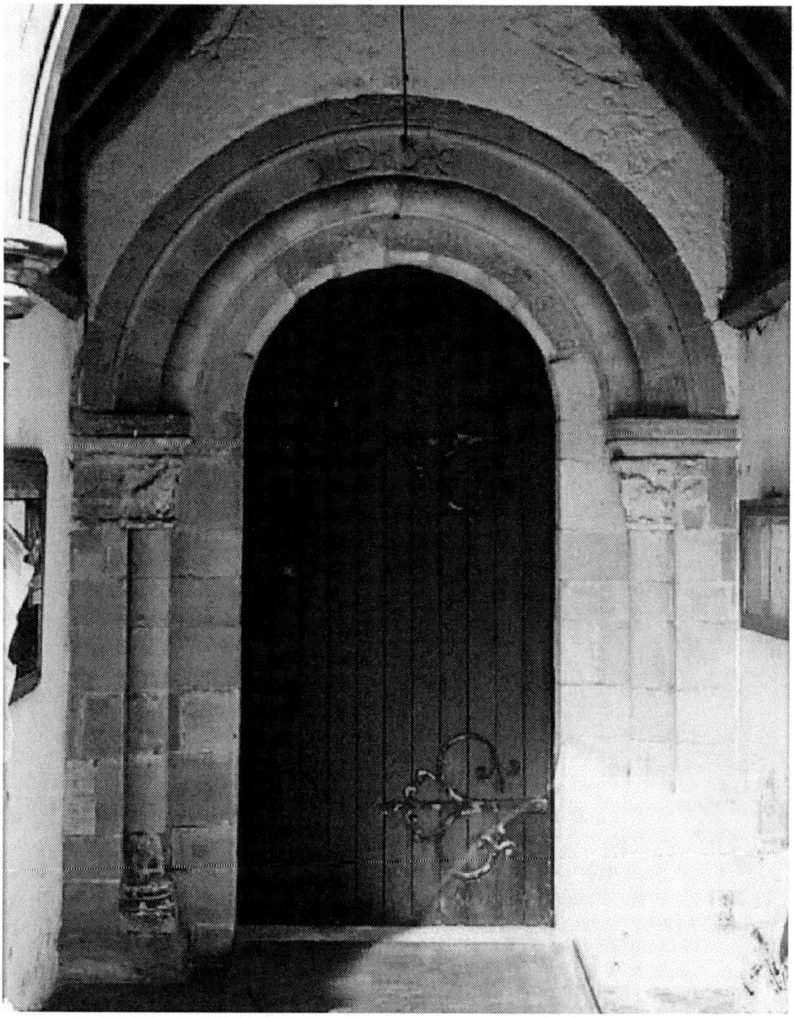

Romanesque south doorway of Great Glen church.

Great Glen
St Cuthbert's church (Landranger Ref. 141:653977) has two Anglo-Saxon carvings in the vestry and a third above the north doorway. The south doorway is Romanesque.

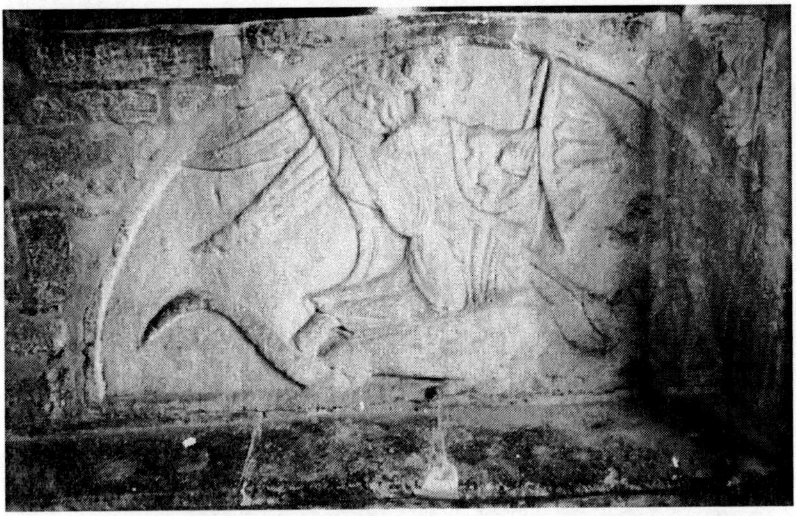

Hallaton's Romanesque tympanum depicting St Michael and a dragon. Barely visible is a small human figure on the right.

Hallaton

Hallaton is often described as the prettiest village in Leicestershire. St Michael and All Angel's church is sited on a spur of hill with a substantial retaining wall about six feet high on the south side (Landranger Ref. 141:786965). The entrance is through the north porch where there is a superb semi-circular Romanesque tympanum (originally situated over a doorway) depicting a large man, a dragon and several smaller figures —generally interpreted as St Michael putting an end to the dragon's inclinations to upset the locals.

On entering the nave, one of the corbels facing the north door in the fourteenth century north aisle depicts a fine green man and several other robust grotesques keep him company. A second green man is on a roof boss in the south aisle.

Also in the south aisle is a magnificent Romanesque font with four carved heads, two human (one a column swallower) and two bestial. It is similar to the font at Greetham.

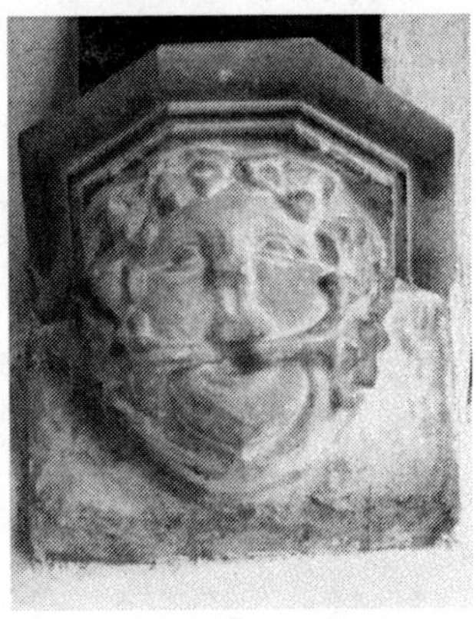

Green man corbel, Hallaton.

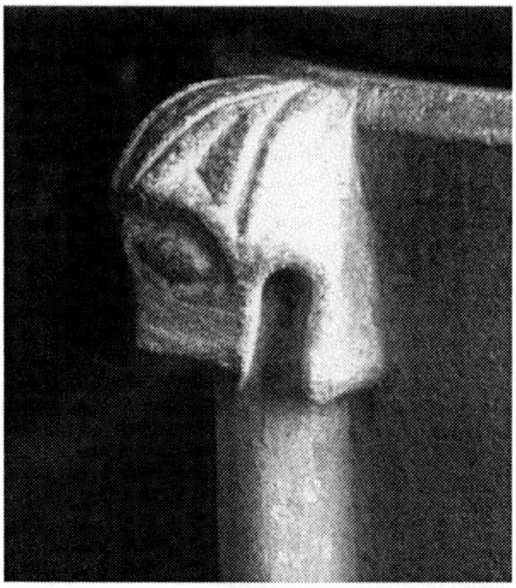

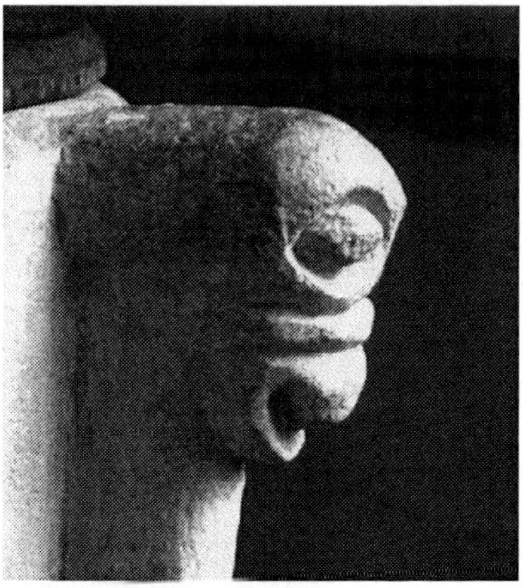

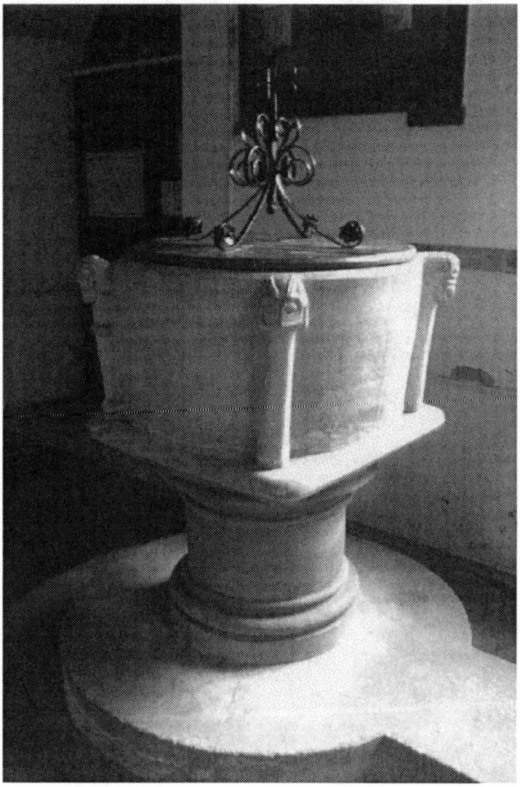

Romanesque font, Hallaton, with close ups of two of the heads.

There are two Anglo-Saxon coffin lids which suggest the even earlier sanctity of the site and confirms the importance of the village a that time, when it was probably an estate centre for the administration of the surrounding forest.

Harston

A substantial fragment of an Anglo-Saxon cross with fine interlace carving stands in St Michael's church porch (Landranger Ref. 130:838318). Further fragments are built into the outside of the east end of the chancel. The building is on a hill top, with good views of Belvoir Castle. It is partially fourteenth century but extensively rebuilt in 1871 and 1888.

Horninghold

St Peter's church (Landranger Ref. 141:807972) has a Romanesque south doorway with a star-type pattern and three demons on the right-hand capital with pointed ears and foliage sprouting from their mouths. A small dragon is on the inside of the left-hand capital. The

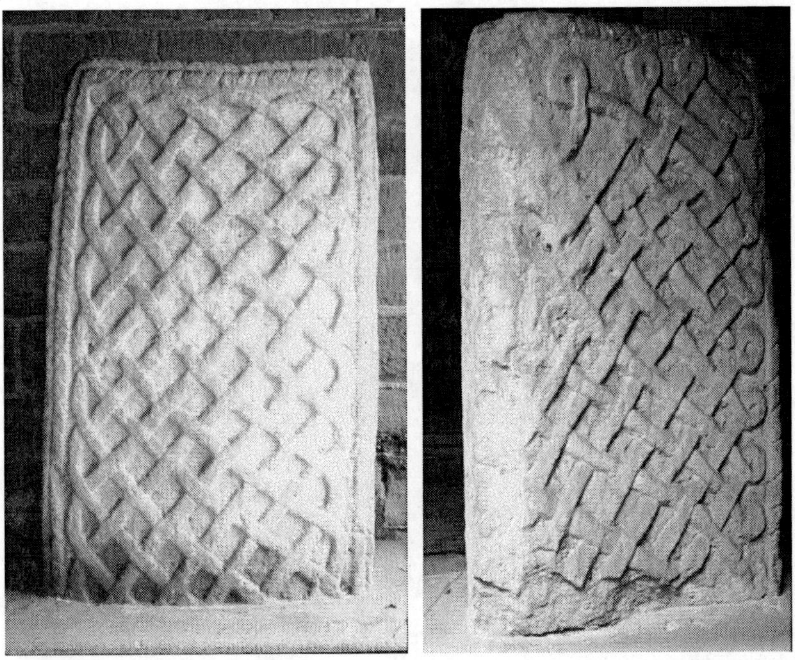

Both sides of one of the Anglo-Saxon cross shaft fragments at Harston.

triple faces on the right-hand capital are in a similar style to carvings from south-central France.

The church is mostly thirteenth century, including the font and probably the spire. The nave has a fine oak roof.

Hose

At the east end of the chancel window in St Michael and All Angels church (Landranger Ref. 129:736293) are two animalistic heads, the right hand one a tongue poker. Inside, the font has four angels

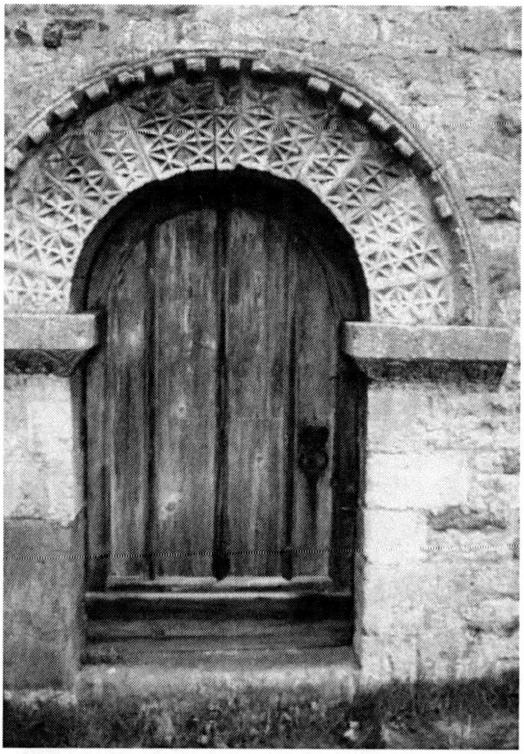

Left: *Romanesque doorway, Horninghold.*

Below: *Detail of right-hand capital with Romanesque green men.*

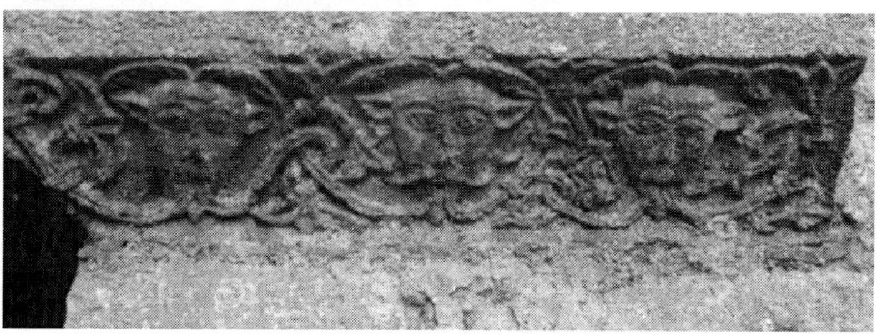

(described some-times as four birds) and between them are four faces, of which two have a sunburst appearance. There are a few other heads and four, fairly recent gargoyles. Much of the church is fourteenth century, although the clerestory is sixteenth century and Anglo-Saxon remains were found when the churchyard was disturbed.

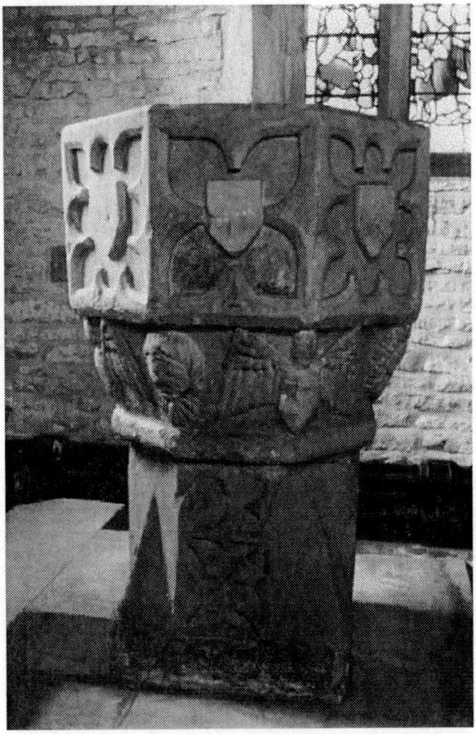

Hose font.

Illston on the Hill

St Michael and All Angels church (Landranger Ref. 141:706994) and the village of Illston are on a prominent hill top. The church was over-restored in 1867. Immediately outside the south door of is the shaft of a medieval cross.

On the outside of the south aisle are three gargoyles depicting fabulous beasties, presumably carved in 1867. Above them on the south wall of the nave are further gargoyles, one of which is gurning. The gargoyle over the blocked north door is in a position similar to a sheela-na-gig.

Inside, the font dates to before the thirteenth century and has faces on

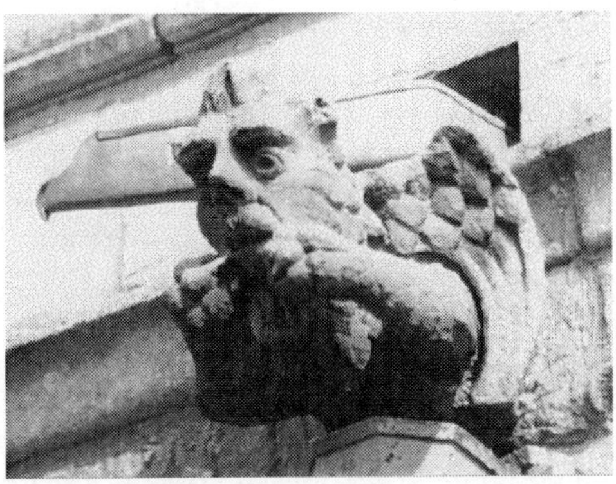

A nineteenth century gurning gargoyle at Illston.

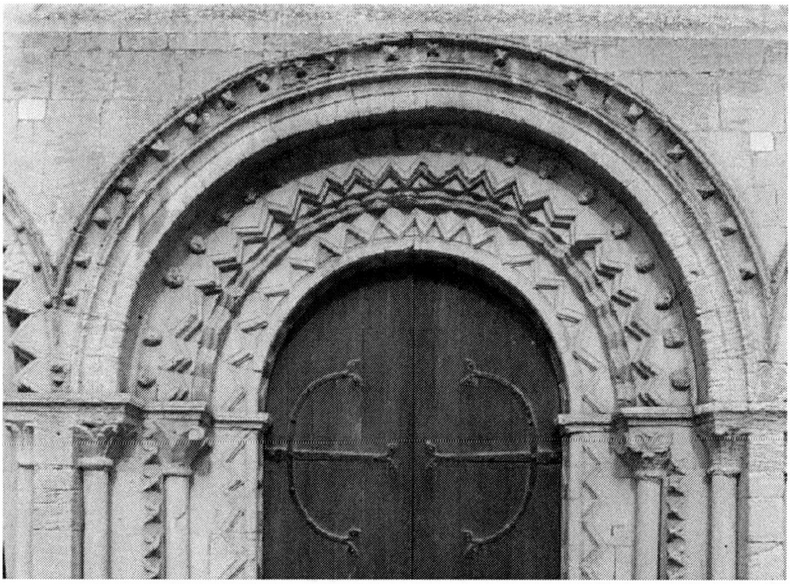

Romanesque south doorway, Ketton.

each corner of the triangular base; there are traces of vesica pisca decoration around the font itself.

Ketton

There is a fragment of an Anglo-Saxon cross in St Mary's church (Landranger Ref. 141:982043). The oldest part of the structure is the Romanesque west doorway. The tower is thirteenth century and the splendid spire fourteenth century. The font is also fourteenth century. The building was restored in 1861.

Although Ketton stone has been widely used for buildings such as the Tower of London, York Minster, Exeter cathedral and many local churches, for some reason Ketton church was constructed of stone from Barnack.

Little Dalby

St James' church (Landranger Ref. 129:775137) is situated away from the village, up a long unmade track. It dates to the thirteenth and fifteenth centuries but was rebuilt in 1851. The base of a medieval cross survives in the churchyard.

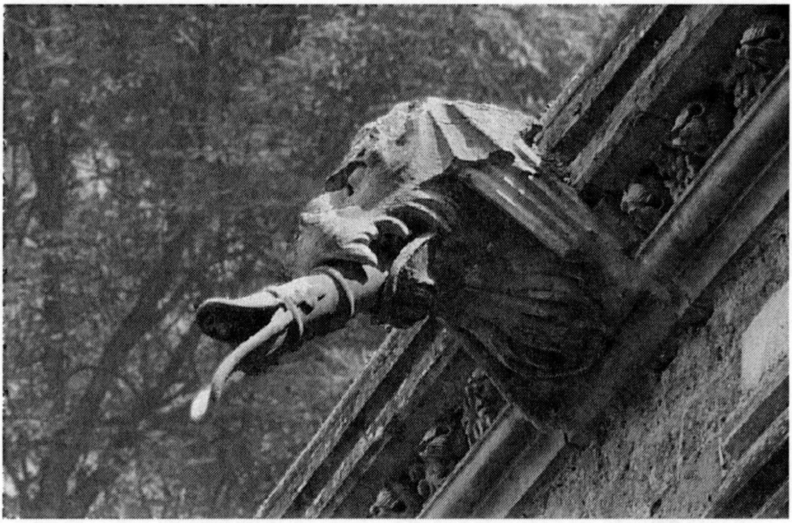

Grotesque gargoyle carved in 1851 at Little Dalby.

Leicester churches

The city of Leicester had a cathedral in the seventh and eighth centuries but, although a Bishop of Leicester was created in AD 679, the Diocese was soon transferred, first to Dorchester and then to Lincoln (probably to avoid problems caused by the Vikings).

St Margaret's (at the end of Church Gate) is almost certainly a late Anglo-Saxon church —perhaps on the site of a Roman cemetery as it is just outside the Roman and medieval city walls. The building that can be seen now has a thirteenth century nave and aisles with a fifteenth century chancel and tower, all restored in the 1860s. There is a twelfth century well at the east end of the north aisle. The wonderful south porch includes a sanctuary ring on the door. Inside are numerous carvings, including green men on the sedilia and behind the altar (see photograph on page 14).

St Mary de Castro's (in Castle Yard) was founded in 1107, possibly on the site of an Anglo-Saxon minster. The surviving building is twelfth century (although over-restored in the 1850s) and includes late Romanesque shafts to the north and south windows. There is a superb Romanesque sedilia and piscina. The altar is also Romanesque (a very rare survival; the only other stone altar of this date in Leicestershire is at Seagrave). The font is thirteenth century and incorporates busts and animals. The building has an unusual structure because what is now the south aisle was built as a separate

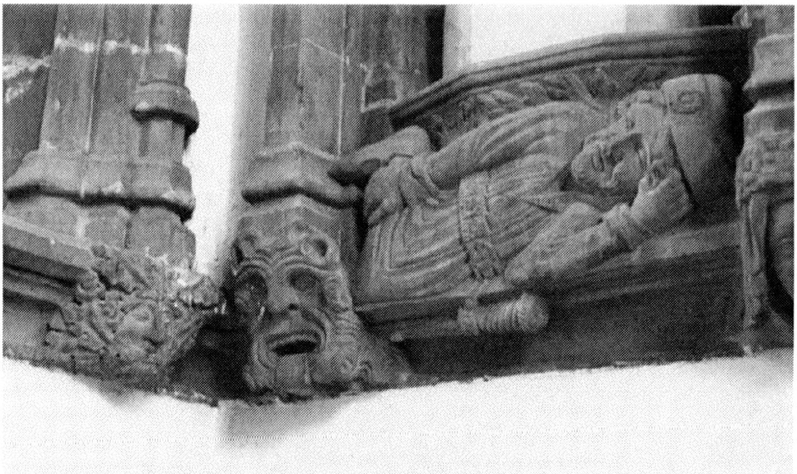

A curious combination of carvings in St Margaret's church, Leicester.

church. The churchyard contains some excellent Swithland slate tombstones.

St Nicholas' (St Nicholas Circle) is a probable early Anglo-Saxon minster too as it (or at least a chapel) was originally dedicated to St Augustine; another chapel (now lost) to the east of the present building was dedicated to St Columban. The nave is mostly early Anglo-Saxon, dating from either the seventh or tenth century, and incorporates re-used Roman tiles. There are the remains of two blocked late Anglo-Saxon windows in the interior of the nave walls.

St Martin's (St Martin's Lane) dates to the twelfth century and became the cathedral in 1927. It is on the site of a Roman columnar building, perhaps a temple, and may have been the site of an Anglo-Saxon church.

All Saints' church (Highcross Street) also may have Anglo-Saxon origins (as do the lost churches of St Peter, St Michael, St Clement and St Leonard). Although the building has a Romanesque west doorway it was mostly built around 1300, with the top of the tower and the battlements built in the fourteenth and fifteenth centuries. The chancel was rebuilt using brick in 1829. The whole building was much restored in 1875. The font is thirteenth century and incorporates busts. There are many fine slate tombstones, including one to John Bracebridge (died 1782) carved by William Firmadge, that includes 'robust' nude angels.

In the nineteenth century the dramatic increase in Leicester's population led to a spate of church-building. The first church to be built in Leicester after the Reformation was St George's (Rutland Street) in 1823 (rebuilt in 1911), followed by Holy Trinity (Regent Road) in 1838 (rebuilt 1871); St John (South Albion Street) in 1854; St Andrew (Jarrom Street) in 1860 and the Roman Catholic's Holy Cross (New Walk) at the turn of the nineteenth and twentieth centuries.

Loddington

St Michael's church (Landranger Ref. 141:786020) is attractively located, with access through a field and trees. There is has a Romanesque doorway and stained glass in the south-east dating from the thirteenth or fourteenth centuries. There is a gurning gargoyle (see photograph on page 8).

Long Clawson

Long Clawson church (Landranger Ref. 129:722272) has a unique dedication —to St Remigius. There are Romanesque pillars in the transept under the central tower. This indicates that the cruciform-plan dates to this period. However most of the church is thirteenth century, with the tower fourteenth century.

On the south porch are two interesting heads — the left-hand one is tongue-poking and the right-hand one is an animal with pointed ears. On the north side of the aisle is a fifteenth or sixteenth century window where the female head is, unusually, on the left. The eight gargoyles round the tower have very round features, rather like so-called 'Celtic' heads.

Inside the north aisle are four heads in a similar style to the porch. Three are animals —one with sprouting foliage, a 'green beast'. The north-west

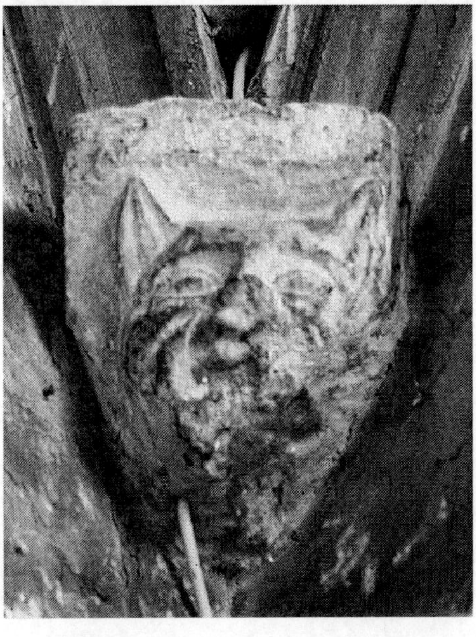

Cat-like springer, Long Clawson.

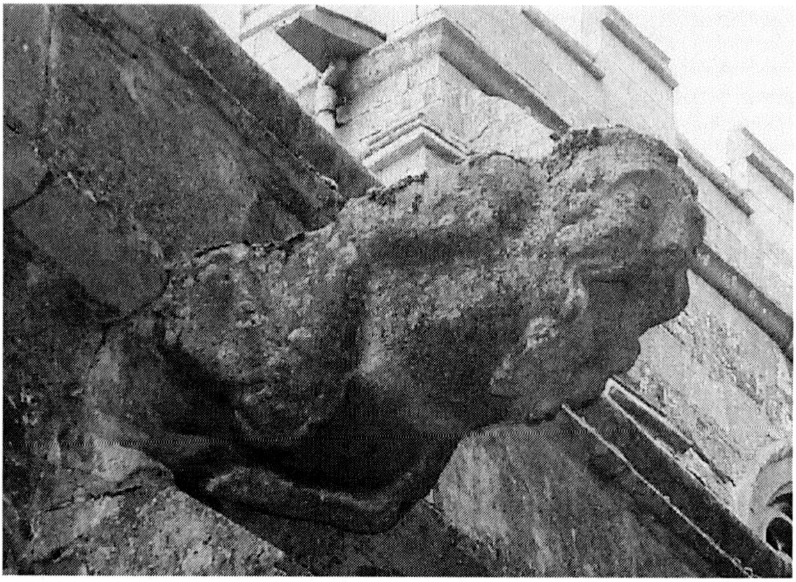

One of the splendid gargoyles on Lowesby church.

one is female, with a square head-dress. There are several foliate carvings on the arch springers with small faces. Inside the central tower crossing are several heads. One is badly defaced, another female and a third with distinctly pointed ears.

Lowesby
All Saints church (Landranger Ref. 141:723074) is set attractively among beeches and chestnuts on a mound falling away to the south. The building is mostly fourteenth century although the south arcade is thirteenth century.

There are friezes of well-sculpted figures around the north and south aisles and the chancel. These include many animal heads, human heads and floral decoration, all very animated. Among them is a dragon. On the tower is a clearly gurning gargoyle and another gurning only with his right hand with the other hand possibly between his legs. On the south aisle is a third gurning gargoyle.

Lubenham
All Saints church (Landranger Ref. 141:705871) was built in the thirteenth and fourteenth centuries (except the tower which is

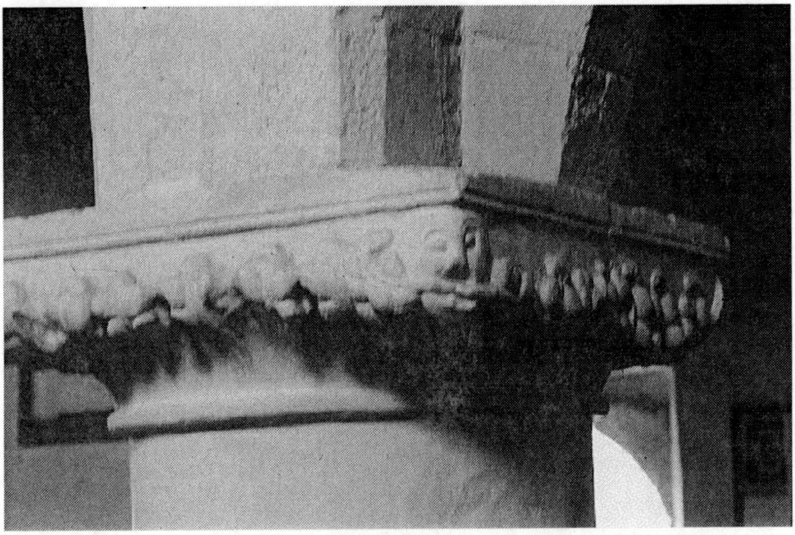

A small green man lurking on a capital at Lubenham

fifteenth century) and has remained unrestored. There are heads on the capitals (including a small green man), chancel arch and the sedilia.

Lutterworth

St Mary's church (Landranger Ref 140:543846) was founded in the twelfth century but the building is mostly thirteenth and fourteenth century. The top of the tower was rebuilt in the eighteenth century after storm damage. The whole church was restored in 1867.

There is a superb gilded green man roof boss at the east end of the nave (see photograph overleaf). A medieval wall painting on the chancel arch depicts the Last Judgement.

Lyddington

St Andrew's church (Landranger Ref 140:877970) has a fourteenth century chancel with earthenware jars in the walls (an early experiment in acoustics); the rest of the building is fifteenth century. There are gurning gargoyles on the tower. Inside are the remains of wall paintings and a wide range of well-carved animal and human grotesques adorning the aisle corbels and nave springers. Such carvings did not cease in the medieval period —at the chancel end of

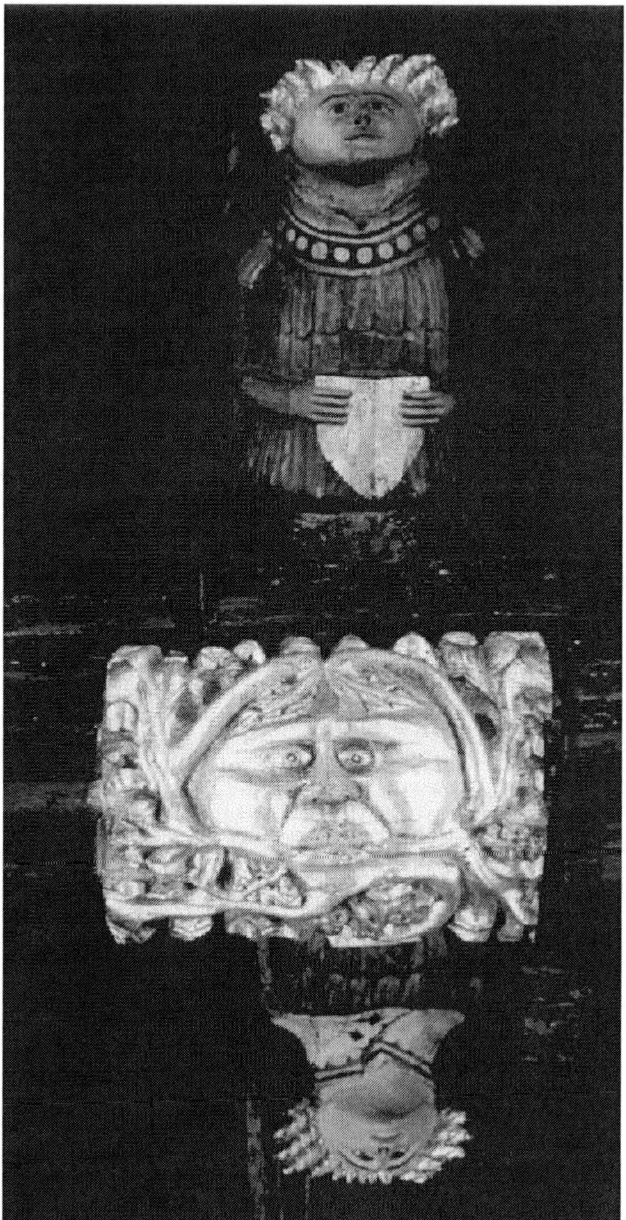

Gilded green man at Lutterworth.

the nave two new carvings (of the bishop and a foliate face) were added in 1991 (see photographs overleaf).

Lyndon

Inside St Martin's church porch (Landranger Ref. 141:907044) is a Romanesque font with serpentine carvings; the rest of the church mostly dates to the fourteenth century. The tasteless alabaster pulpit and reredos date from the restoration of 1866. There are rood loft stairs, miserable-looking faces in the springers of the nave arcade, and a three-eyed face decorating the south porch doorway. On the outside are well-sculpted gargoyles (see photograph overleaf)..

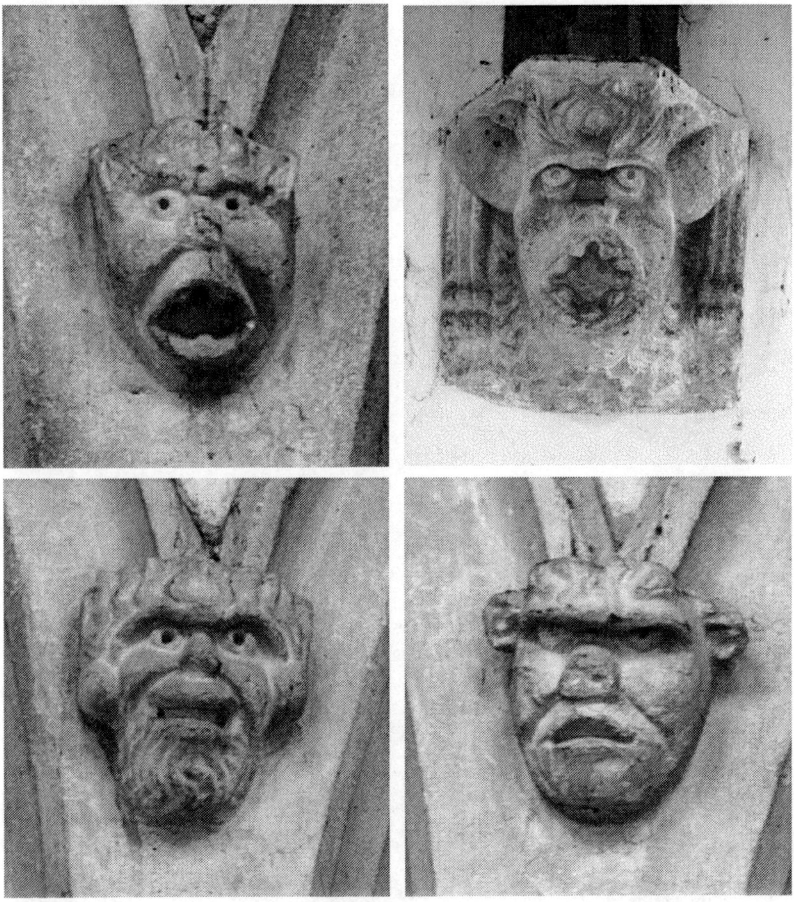

Medieval carvings in Lyddington church (see also photograph on page 9).

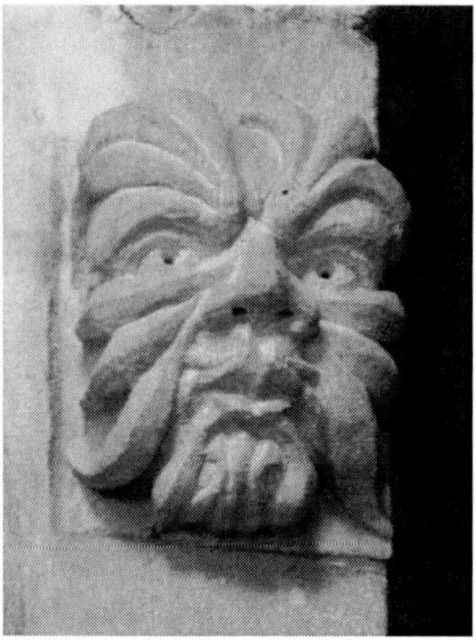

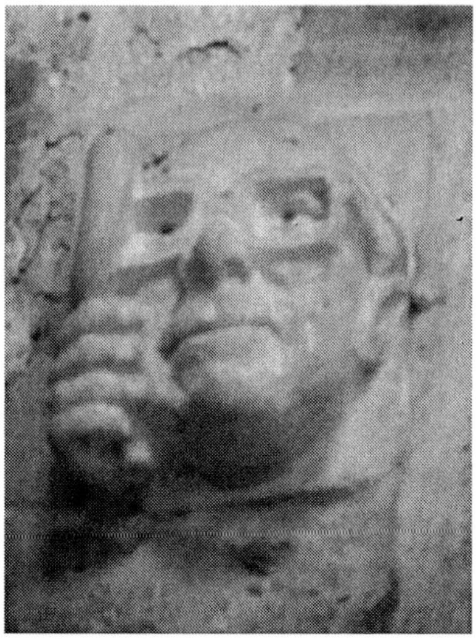

The foliate face and bishop in Lyddington church carved in 1991.

Market Harborough

The parish church is dedicated to St Dionysius (Landranger Ref. 141: 733873). It dates to the fourteenth and fifteenth centuries and has a superb broached steeple.

The ruined church of St Mary in Arden (Landranger Ref. 141: 740874) incorporates a Romanesque doorway decorated with twenty-two 'beaked heads' (see photograph on page 7). It was rebuilt in 1693 from a much larger gale-wrecked predecessor dating from

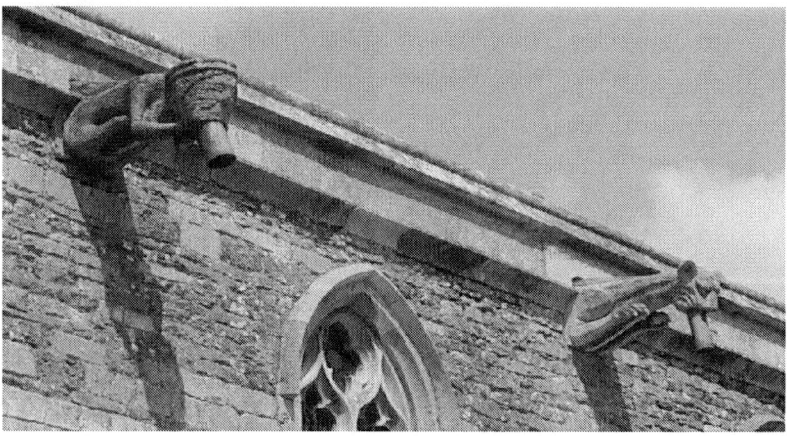

Gargoyles on Lyndon church.

about 1100. Inside the south porch is a fourteenth century female effigy. A large Anglo-Saxon cremation cemetery was discovered in the churchyard in 1799. There are many excellent slate tombstones in the churchyard.

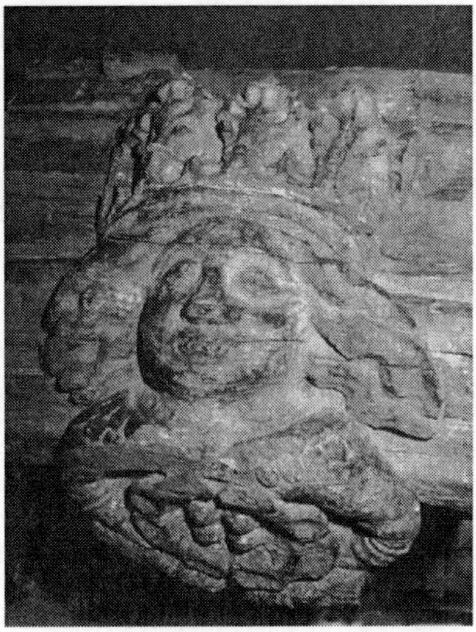

A roof boss removed from St Dionysius, Market Harborough and now in Market Harborough Museum. Reproduced by kind permission of Leicestershire County Council Heritage Services.

Manton

St Mary's church (Landranger Ref. 141:881047) is mostly Romanesque but, apart from the tower, rebuilt in the fourteenth century. The decorated capitals and font are Romanesque. There is a medieval stone coffin lid decorated with an attractive cross. In the very attractive churchyard are many tombstones. One is said to be decorated with mermaids, but this is incorrect — these are especially florid depictions of the soul of the deceased; simpler versions have been dubbed 'Belvoir Angels'.

Market Overton

SS Peter and Paul's church (Landranger Ref 130:885165) is on the site of an Anglo-Saxon cemetery. Two substantial fragments of Anglo-Saxon cross shafts are built into the base of the tower. Fragments of Anglo-Saxon columns (possibly reused Roman columns) adorn the stile to the north of the churchyard. The sundial was reputedly donated by Sir Isaac Newton (his mother or grandmother was from Market Overton).

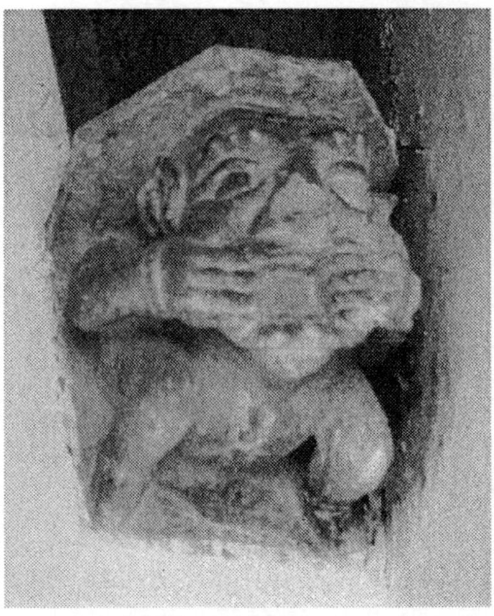

Gurning corbel, Manton.

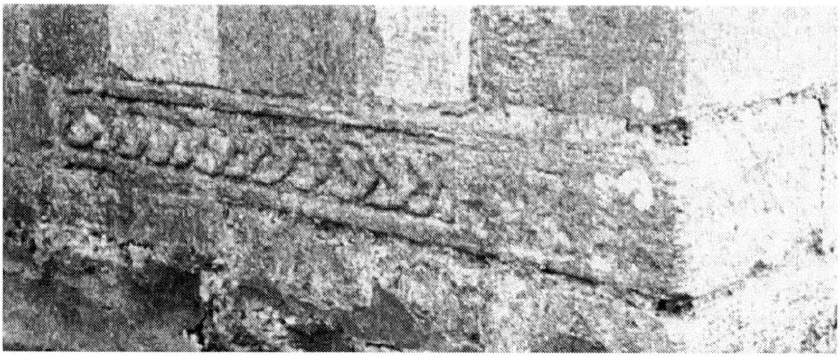

One of two fragments of Anglo-Saxon cross shaft incorporated into the base of the church tower at Market Overton.

Inside, the tower arch is Anglo-Saxon (the only worthwhile piece of Anglo-Saxon architecture in the county in Pevsner's opinion) and reuses Roman masonry, as does the odd font base (although this is probably Romanesque rather than Anglo-Saxon). The church door and ironwork dates to the early fourteenth century. The nave is later fourteenth century.

Morcott

St Mary's is the most complete Romanesque church in Rutland (Landranger Ref. 141:924007). There is an unsullied Romanesque arcade that includes carved capitals of great interest; the human and animal heads have growing from them stylised fir-cones, the well-known symbol of fecundity that evolved into the 'pineapples' so beloved as finials for gateposts. Another capital shows an orobus —a snake biting its own tail. Although these capitals are now bare stone we should bear in mind that originally they would have been elaborately painted.

The lower parts of the tower and the south doorway are also Romanesque. There are also fragments of Anglo-Saxon masonry in the tower. The fifteenth century chancel retains a thirteenth century arch and fourteenth century tomb. The pulpit is a beautiful example of Jacobean (seventeenth century) wood carving.

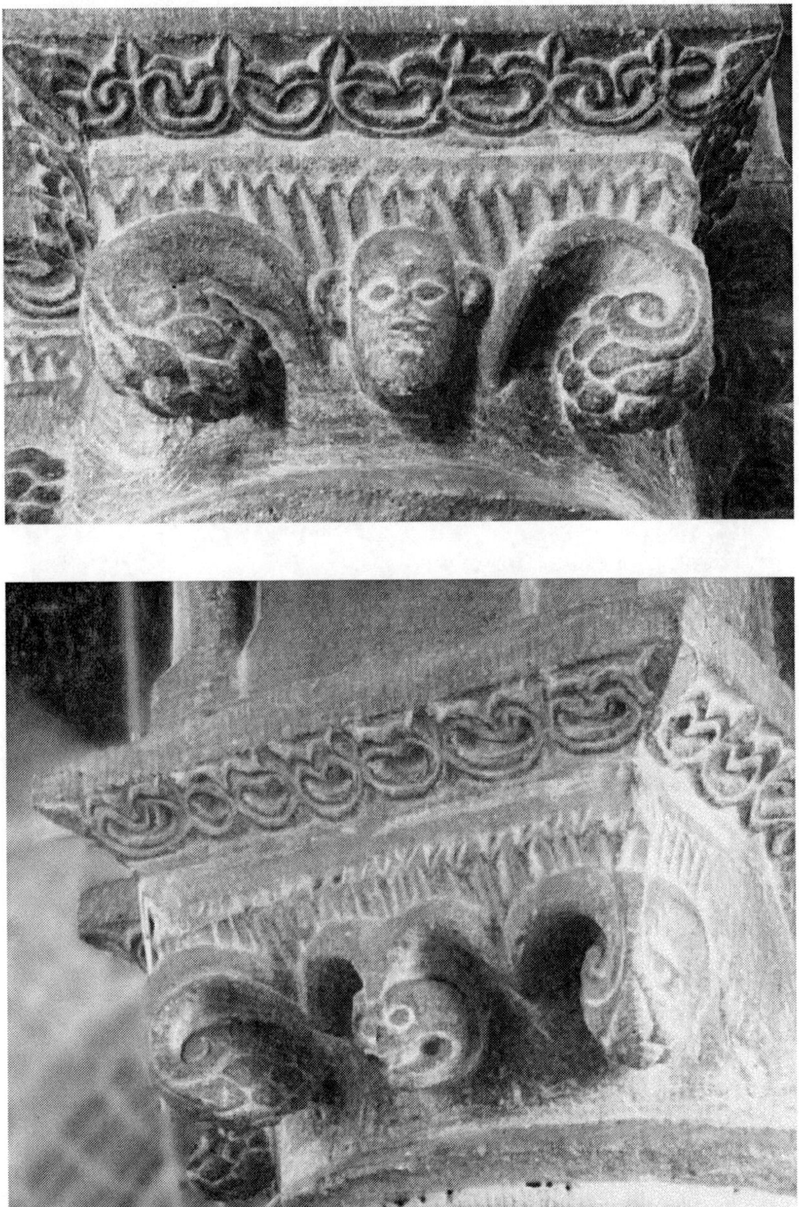

Two Romanesque capitals in the north arcade of Morcott church.

Mountsorrel

The medieval lantern cross was removed to Swithland in 1793 by Sir John Danvers, the then owner of Swithland Hall, and the present domed Butter Market built in its place (Landranger Ref. 129:580148). A replica of the original cross was carved by Mike Grevatte (who lived in Mountsorrel at the time) and erected in 1994 a few hundred yards to the north.

St Peter's church is the 'north end' church (Landranger Ref. 129:580148) and has four

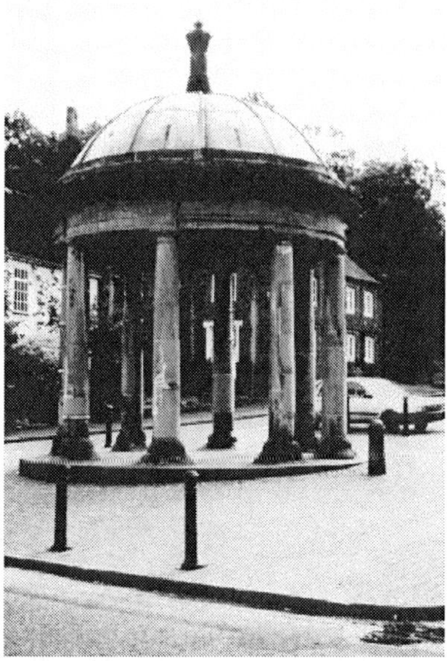

Top right: *The Butter Cross at Mountsorrel, built 1793.*
Below left: *The replacement cross at Mountsorrel.*
Below right: *Detail of the 'lantern'.*

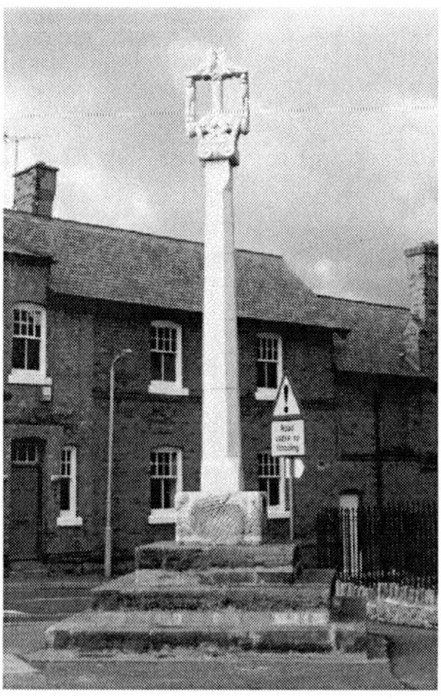

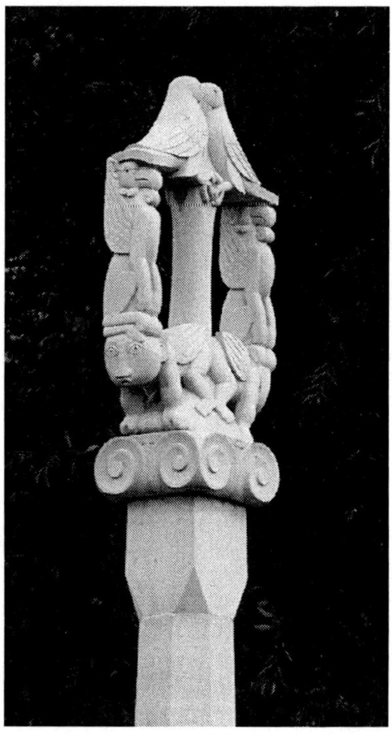

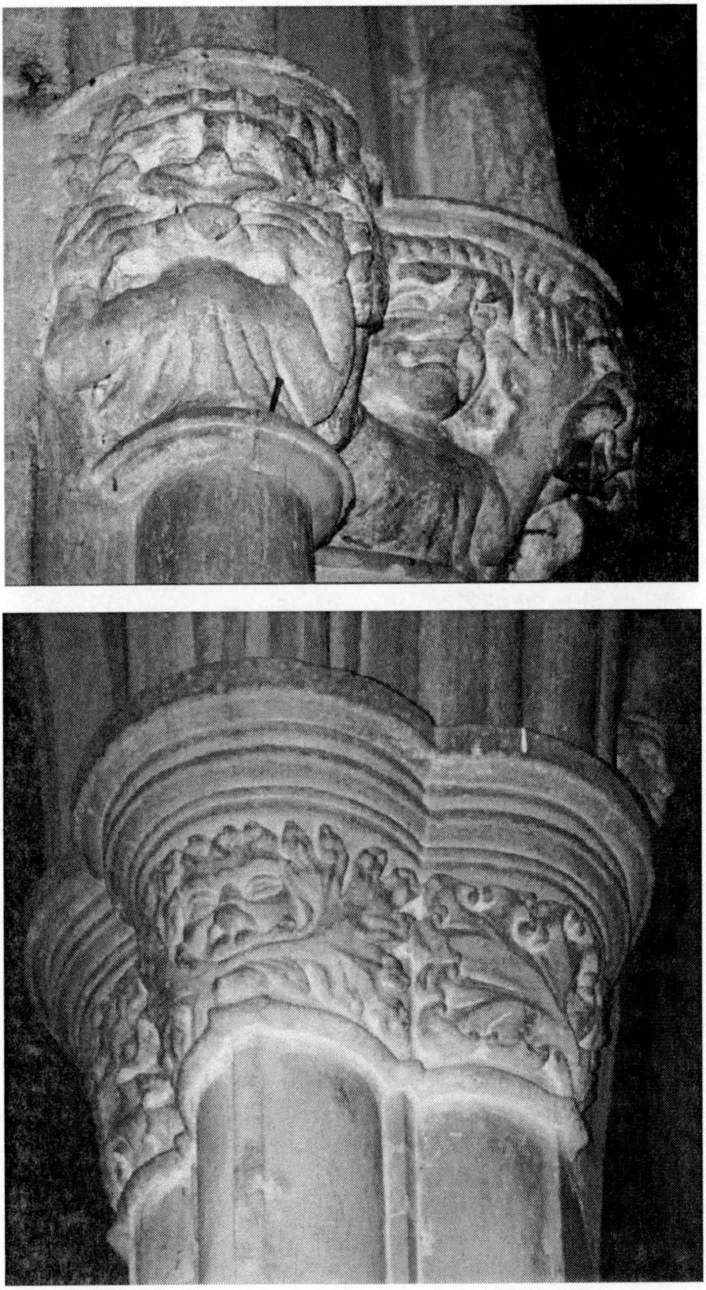

Fourteenth century capitals in All Saints', Oakham.

gargoyles on the tower; the north-west one is gurning. It was rebuilt about 1800, retaining an older tower. The second church, Christ Church, was built in 1844.

Oakham

All Saints' church (Landranger Ref. 141:861089) has early fourteenth century nave arcades with unusual carved capitals including a dragon and a green man (see photograph on previous page). There is also a figure in the chancel arch. On the exterior there are many carvings; two gargoyles on the north side of the tower are gurning. The weathervane, known as 'Cock Peter', is one of the oldest in England and probably dates back to the fourteenth century.

The nearby Castle is the largest and best-preserved of all the Norman great halls. It was built between 1180 and 1190 for Walkelin de Ferrers and is the earliest surviving secular building in Britain. Inside are various Romanesque carvings, including paired heads and six musicians. Possibly they were carved by the same mason responsible for the capitals of the chancel at Canterbury Cathedral.

Most of the rest of the castle was ruinous by the early sixteenth century (the foundations are under the grass) but the great hall remained in use as a courtroom. Although not used for assize courts since 1970, monthly magistrates' courts and occasional crown courts are still held here.

The castle is also home to the better-known collection of ornamental horseshoes. There are over 200 of these, deriving from a custom dating back to at least 1521 (but probably to several centuries before that) requiring any peer of the realm to donate a horseshoe or pay a fine when they first travel through Oakham. The oldest may date from about 1470. The custom is maintained and the collection include horseshoes presented by Queen Elizabeth II, Princess Margaret and the Duke of Gloucester. The most recent is that given by the Princess Royal in 1999.

Owston

St Andrew's church (Landranger Ref. 141:774080) is situated on a mound and dates to about 1160. The north and south doorways are both Romanesque. The font is also twelfth century. There are some excellent foliate roof bosses. Outside, there are two gargoyles on the north aisle, one gurning. Also there is a fairly recent (probably nineteenth century) corbel head with exaggerated asymmetrical features.

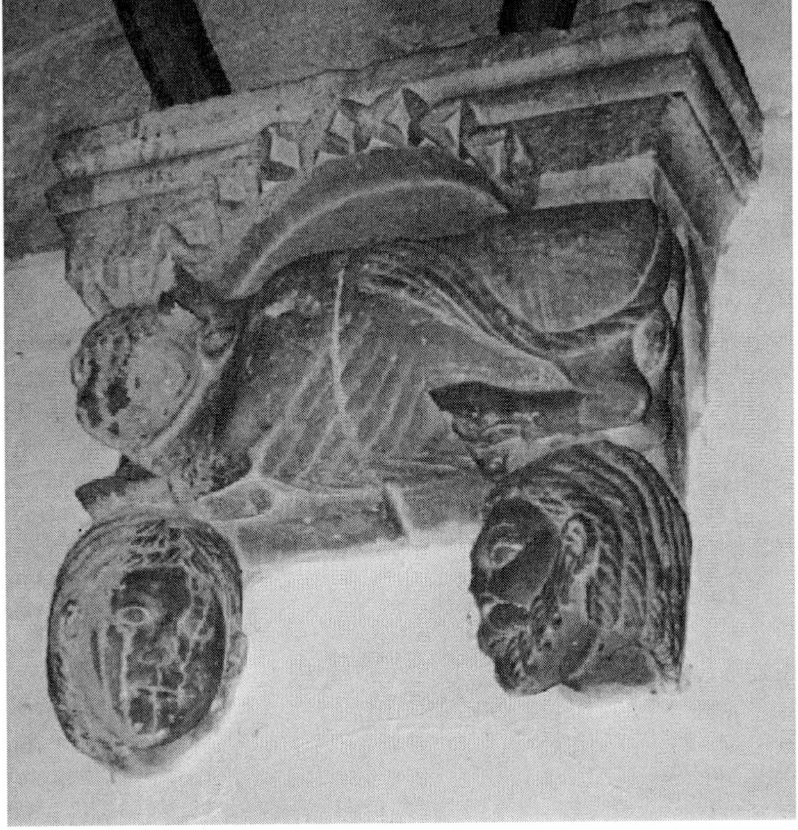

Romanesque carving inside Oakham Castle.

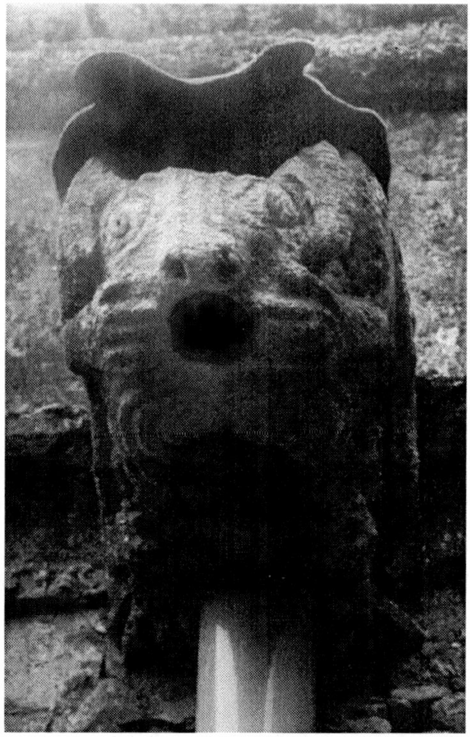

Gurning gargoyle, Owston church.

It was founded as an Augustinian priory; monastic earthworks, mostly fishponds, lie to the south. The surviving building is only a small part of the original monastic complex. Cloisters and other buildings were probably demolished soon after the Dissolution but, until at least 1730, a large gateway still survived by the road to the north of the church.

Queniborough

St Mary's church (Landranger Ref. 129: 651120) has a Romanesque window in the chancel and thirteenth century arcades. The spire is exceptionally slender and needle-like.

The wooden roof incorporates some excellent roof bosses, including a bearded 'tricephalous' (three-heads-in-one) face, an ithyphallic ('X-rated') male contortionist, and a tongue-poking animal.

Ridlington

SS Mary and Andrew's church (Landranger Ref. 141:847027) has an approximately semi-circular Romanesque tympanum now situated over the vestry door. It depicts two mythical beasts, one winged, and an eight-spoked wheel (see photograph on page 72). The font is three-sided. The building is mostly thirteenth century but was severely restored in 1858.

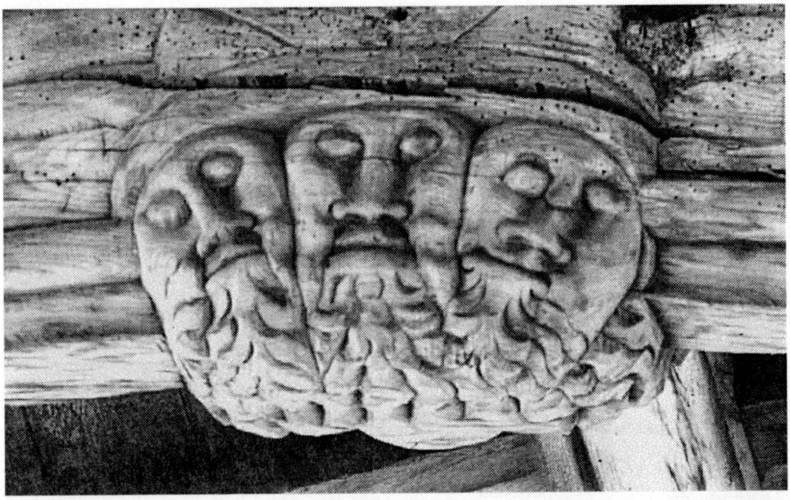

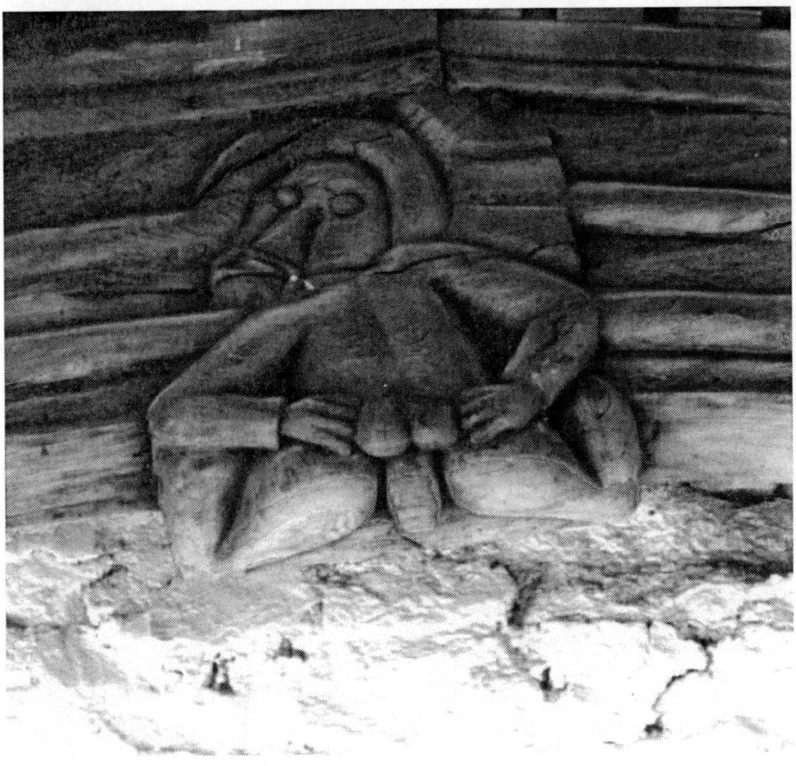

Roof bosses in Queniborough church.

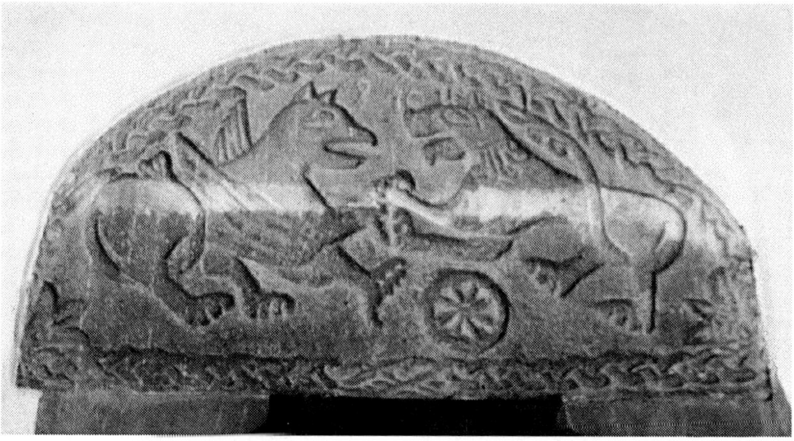

Ridlington tympanum.

Rothley

The parish church of SS Mary and John the Baptist (Landranger Ref. 129:585126) is thirteenth century, except for the chancel which was rebuilt in 1878. The grotesque beasts on the exterior appear to date from the nineteenth century too.

In the churchyard is the county's largest surviving Anglo-Saxon cross shaft, although it is not complete as the head is missing. This is almost certainly the best physical evidence we have for Rothley being a site of regional importance in the early Christian period.

Also in the churchyard there is also a famous slate tombstone showing the Last Judgement taking place in Swithland churchyard (carved by John Hind in memory of William Hunt who died in 1794).

Ryhall

St John the Evangelist's church (Landranger Ref. 130:036108) has a thirteenth century tower and spire, chancel arch and nave arch. The sedilia is fourteenth century. There are many heads on the external friezes including a 'green animal' on the north aisle, and a multitude of green men, gurning faces, tongue-pokers, dragons and other mythical animals.

Scalford

The church (Landranger Ref. 129:763242) is dedicated to St Egelwin the Martyr —the only dedication to this seventh century saint in the

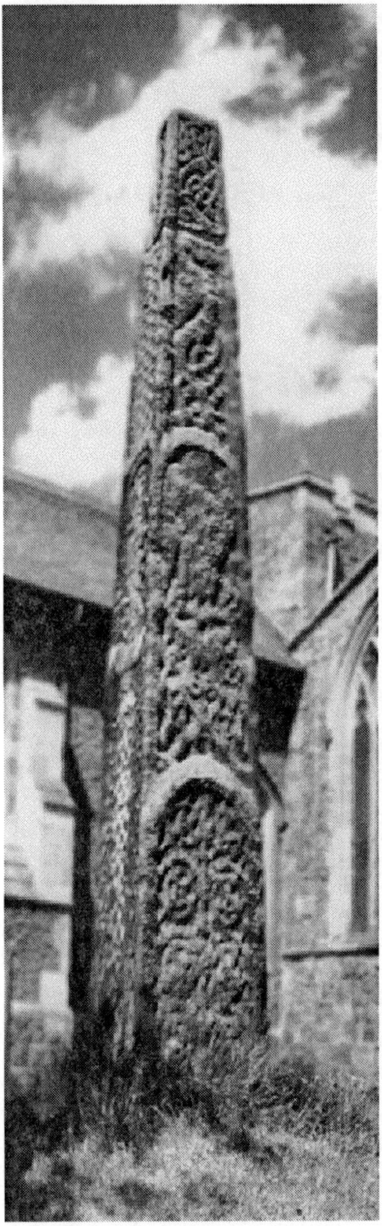

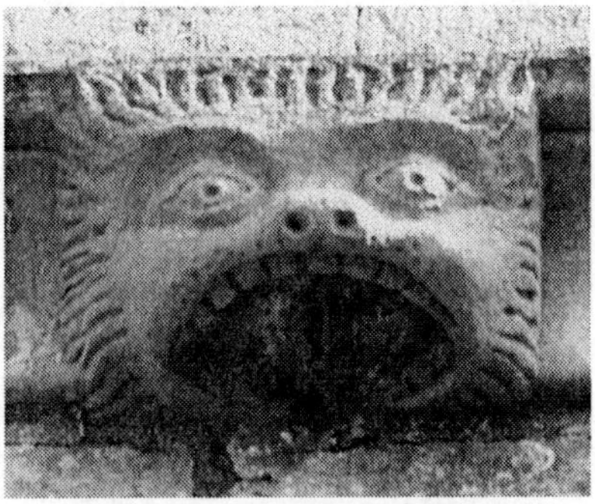

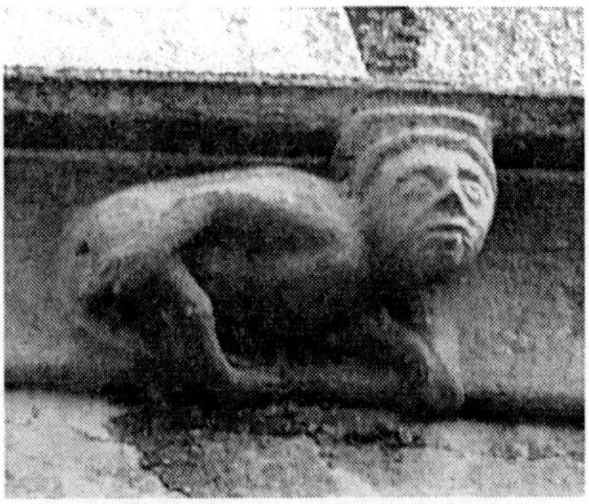

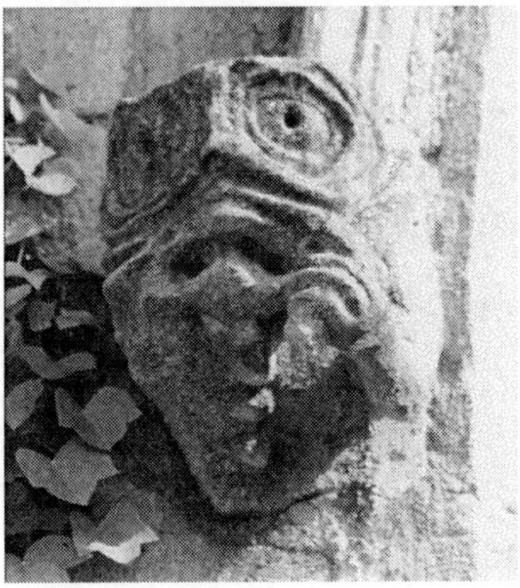

Anglo-Saxon cross shaft in Rothley churchyard.

Carvings on Ryhall church (see also photograph on page 13).

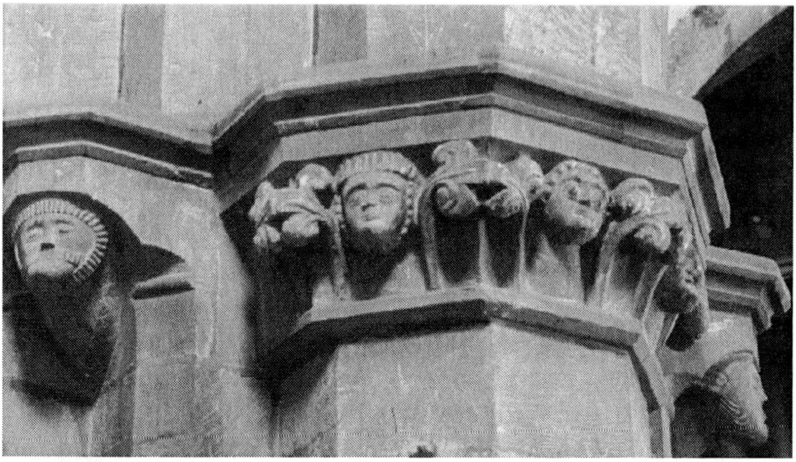

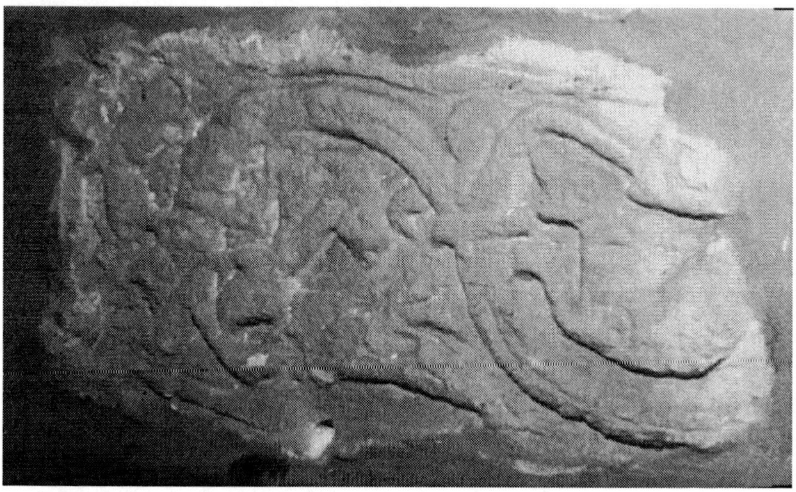

Top: *Thirteenth century capital, Scalford church. The face on the left is wearing a 'scold's bridle'.*
Bottom: *Anglo-Scandinavian carving, Scalford church.*

country. The building is thirteenth and fourteenth century, with a seventeenth century tower with gurning gargoyles.

The foliate roof bosses and decorative heads are of special interest; in the roof of the porch is a boss depicting a tongue-poking green man. Other carvings of interest include thirteenth century carved heads in the chancel arch capitals (including what appears to be a 'scold's bridle' —an instrument of punishment inflicted on

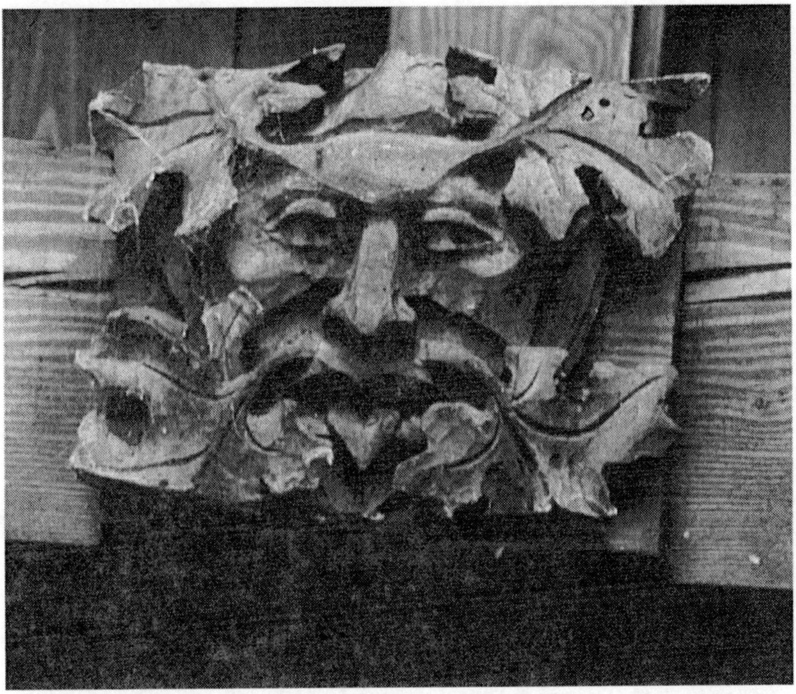

Splendid wooden Green Man in the porch of Scalford church.

women who were considered to nag their husbands too often) and a small green man on the corner of the frieze. An unusual Anglo-Scandinavian carving can be seen by the rood loft stairs (almost behind the pulpit).

There is the base of a circular medieval cross in the churchyard.

Seaton

All Hallows church (Landranger Ref. 141:904893) has capitals in the chancel arch that show a strong affinity with the well-known vegetation carvings in Southwell Minster (Nottinghamshire). There is a late Romanesque doorway with defaced heads (see photograph overleaf). The chancel arch and arcades are also twelfth century. There is a sedilia, piscina and aumbry (still with doors). The reredos is nineteenth century. An ancient font has been converted into a seat. The old parish chest survives. The tower and spire are fourteenth century. There are ancient tombstones on the outer walls.

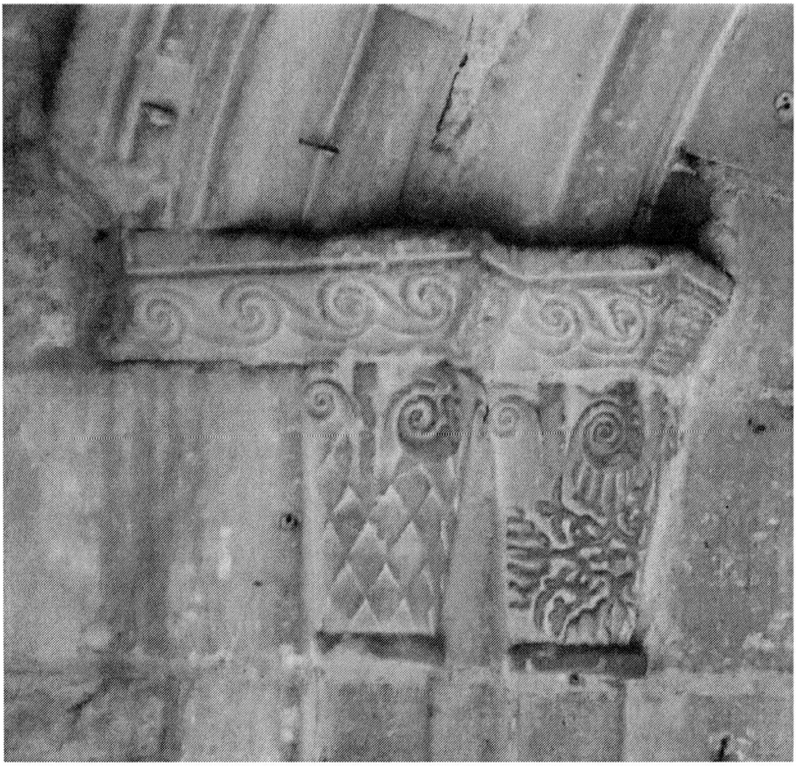

Part of the south doorway of Seaton church.

Shearsby

The church of St Mary Magdelene (Landranger Ref. 140:623910) has dragons and gargoyles on the exterior. Two half-dragon/half-frog grotesques are by the altar. An ancient wooden statue of St Mary Magdalene stands in the chancel. The screen was originally in Knaptoft church. The tower, with its curious octagonal cap, was built in 1789 —and the rest was rebuilt in the nineteenth century, reusing the original sedilia and piscina.

Sileby

The nave corbels in St Mary's church (Landranger Ref. 129:600152) include an asymmetrical face with the mouth twisted to one side and a tongue-poker. There is an excellent green man on a roof boss in the nave. The font is thirteenth century, as are the nave arches. The rest is mostly fifteenth century. Two gargoyles on the tower have lead spouts shaped into toothed snakes' heads.

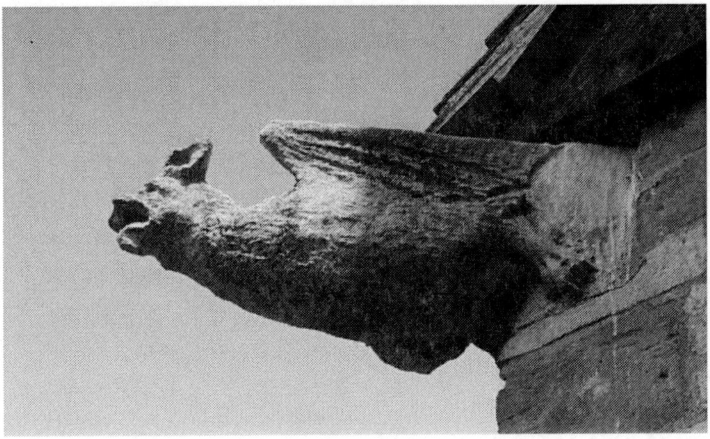

Nineteenth century gargoyle on Shearsby church.

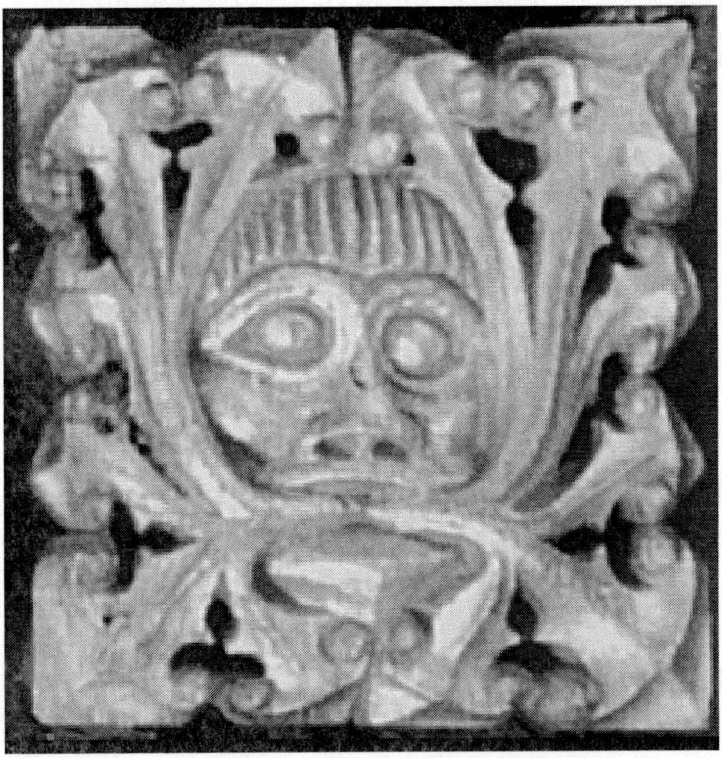

Green man roof boss, Sileby. Photo by Ruth Wylie.

South Croxton
St John the Baptist's church (Landranger Ref. 129:692103) has a gurning gargoyle on west side of south aisle. On the tower the west gargoyle is gurning (see photograph on page xii) and the east one almost so —the hands are on its cheeks rather than in its mouth. The gargoyle on the south of the tower is in the form of a harnessed bear. Inside, the font is Romanesque and decorated with an arcade and one moustachioed face. The building dates from about 1300 to 1350.

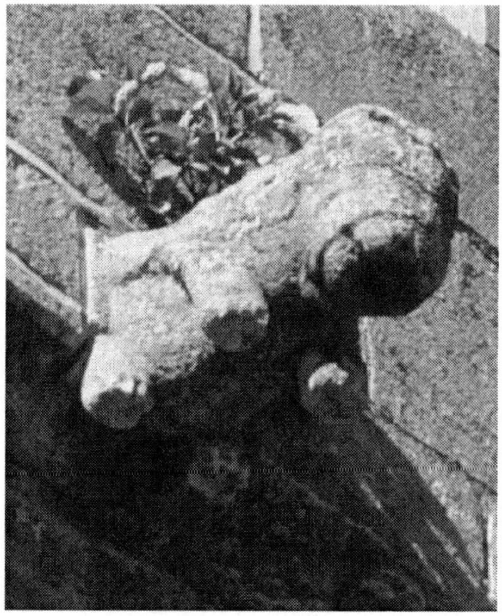

Bear gargoyle on South Croxton church.

Sproxton
St Batholomew's church (Landranger Ref. 130:857249) stands on a hilltop away from the present village (although earthworks suggest that an earlier settlement was close to the church).

On the tower are four gargoyles; the north-east one is a griffin-like animal with 'bug' eyes that is gurning (see photograph on page 11). On the vestry is a tongue-poker with pointed eyes; probably of nineteenth century date.

In the nave are sixteen superb corbel heads. On the north side three have hare-like pointed ears; one of these is gurning, another tongue-poking. One is a dragon and there is a beaked head. In the south-east corner is a either a hedgehog or an owl.

Little known but of great importance are the six superb wooden carvings of green men and foliate faces forming the bases of the wall plates for the roof beams in the south aisle. One has foliage sprouting from the eyes as well as the mouth.

Although technically a 'fragment', as the lower part is missing, the most complete Anglo-Saxon cross in Leicestershire now stands in Sproxton churchyard (see photograph on page 4). More correctly, this cross should be termed 'Anglo-Norse' as the design is similar to

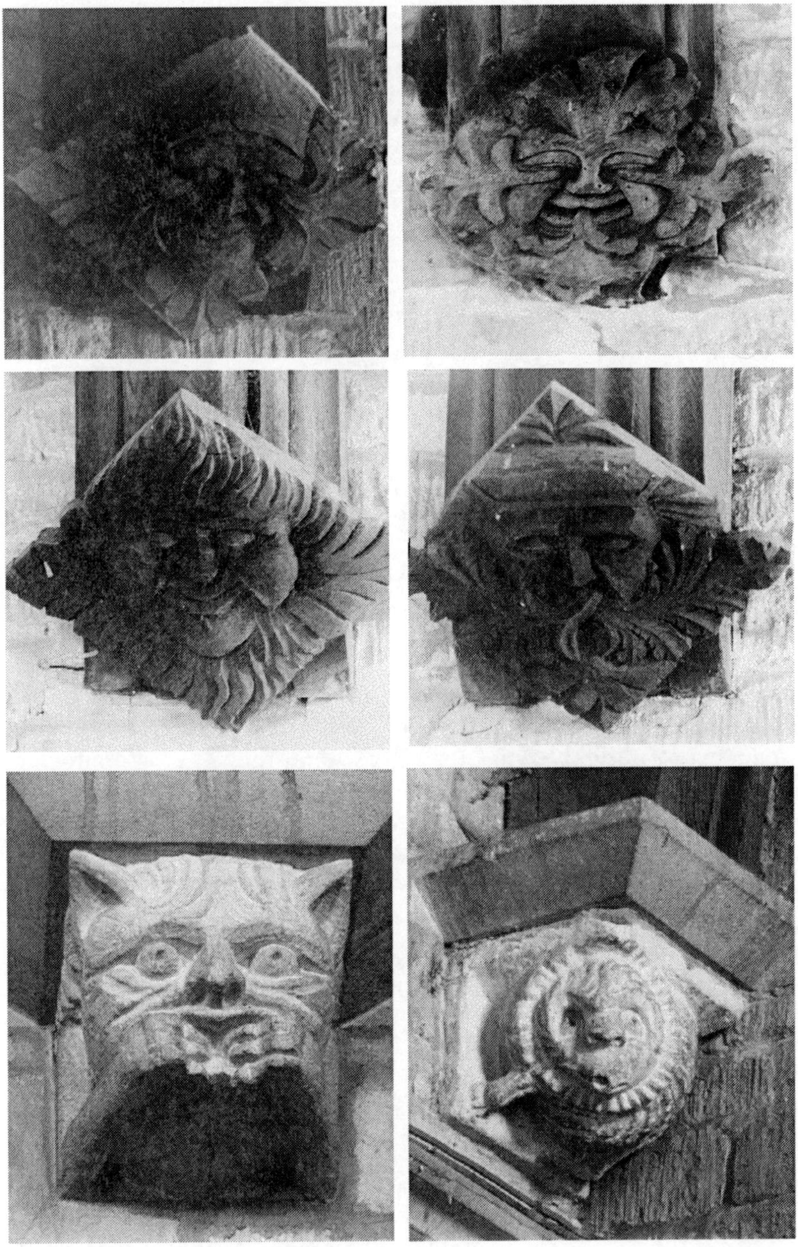

Wooden Green Men and stone corbels in Sproxton church (see also photograph on page 11..

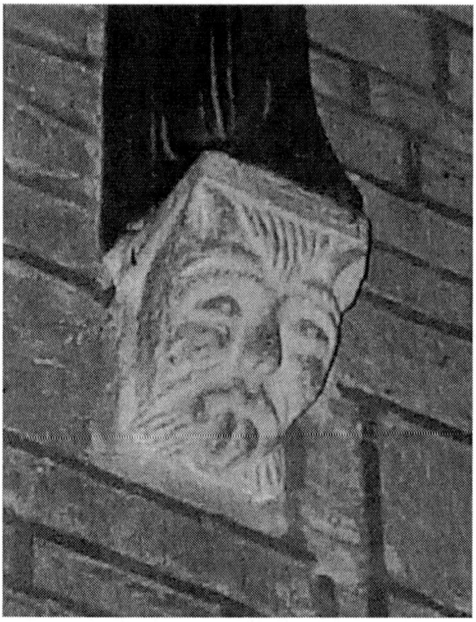

Corbel in the nave of Stathern church.

crosses carved in areas, such as the Isle of Man, settled by Norwegians rather than Saxons. It dates to about the tenth century and was used as a footbridge for over 400 years (which is why one face is almost worn away) until being re-erected in the twentieth century. The cross was not necessarily originally intended for this church and may have been a boundary marker for the lands of the minster at Buckminster.

Stathern

St Guthlac's church (Landranger Ref. 129: 773309) contains fragments of Anglo-Saxon masonry. One doorway is thirteenth century and the font is fourteenth century. The current entrance is from the north, although the south entrance is more imposing. There are gargoyles on the tower, one of which is gurning, and another in a position akin to so-called sheela-na-gigs or female exhibitionists.

Inside there are some interesting carved heads on the nave corbels —two have hare-like ears, and the one nearest the chancel is pulling a face, but without using his hands, so is not strictly gurning. Note that the north side figures are all male and the south side all female.

Stoke Dry

In St Andrew's church (Landranger Ref. 141:856967) the Romanesque columns of the chancel arch are famous for their carvings of a multitude of animals and humans. The whole is very confused but worthy of spending time to allow motifs to become clear. They include dragons, green men, and what may be a mermaid. One of the notable depictions is a bell ringer pulling on a

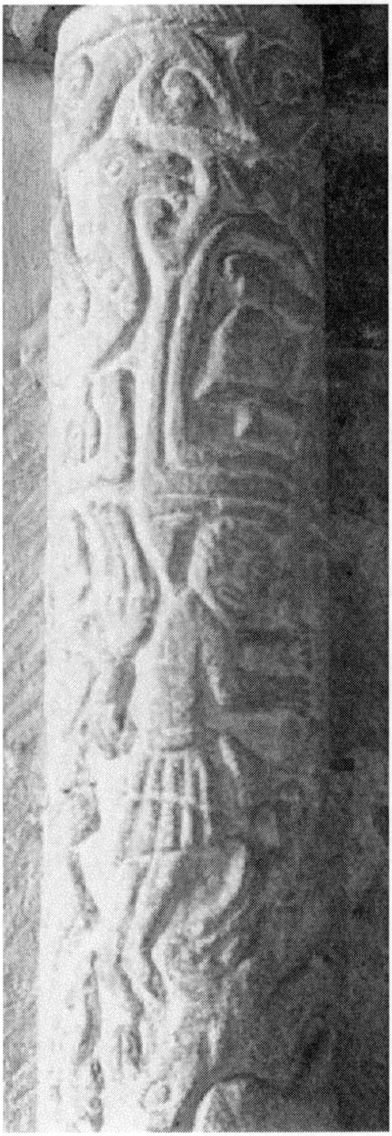

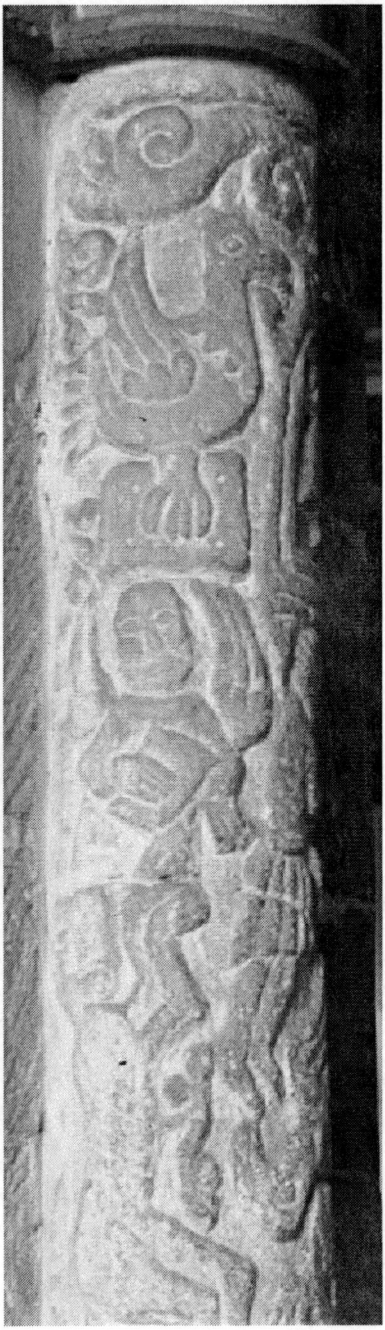

Romanesque columns, Stoke Dry church; note bell ringer (above.)

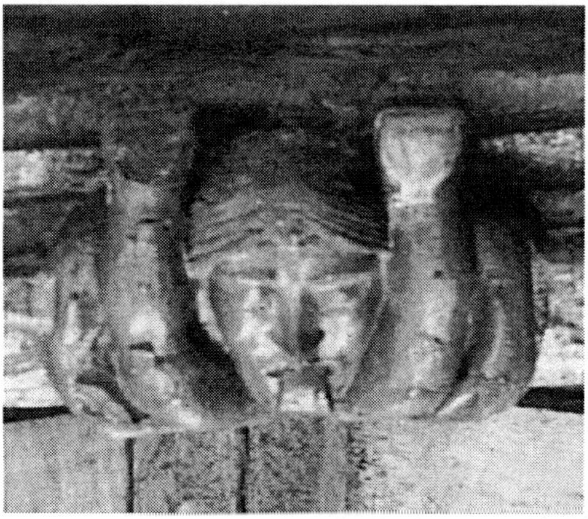

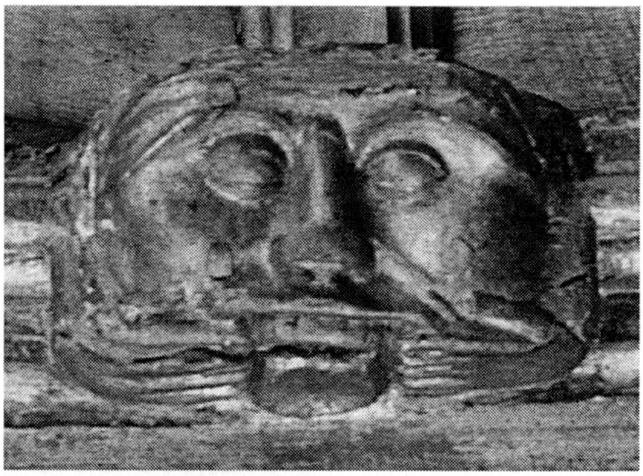

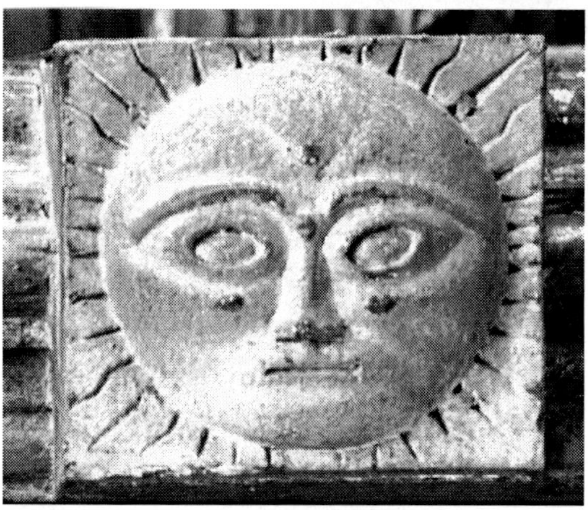

Roof bosses in Stoke Golding church.

rope 'sally'; this must be one of the earliest depictions of such activities.

There is also a Romanesque string course in the chancel with tendrils, animals and humans, and a thirteenth century tower. Much of the rest of the church dates to the fifteenth century. The pre-Reformation rood screen survives, although not without damage.

Stoke Golding

St Margaret's church (Landranger Ref. 140: 398973) is a beautiful church. The font dates to about 1330 and has depictions of St Margaret and a dragon, St Cather-ine and her wheel; another saint (perhaps Nicholas); and a bishop.

The wooden roof bosses are fascinating, too. In the south aisle is a tongue-poker with his head between his legs and another almost-gurning face. One of the most striking is a gilded 'sunburst'. The remaining bosses are foliate.

The real splendours, however, are the capitals of the south aisle arcade. These date from about 1280 to 1290 and are decorated with multiple faces, foliate heads, even a lady in a wimple, all amidst a forest of foliage. Perhaps the most intriguing are a sideways face with big hare-like ears and a tongue-poker.

Stoney Stanton

Outside St Michael's church (externally rebuilt in the nineteenth century; Landranger Ref. 140: 489948), above the priest's door on the north side of the chancel, is a semi-circular Romanesque tympanum with several beasts, a large bird (maybe a raven or dove)

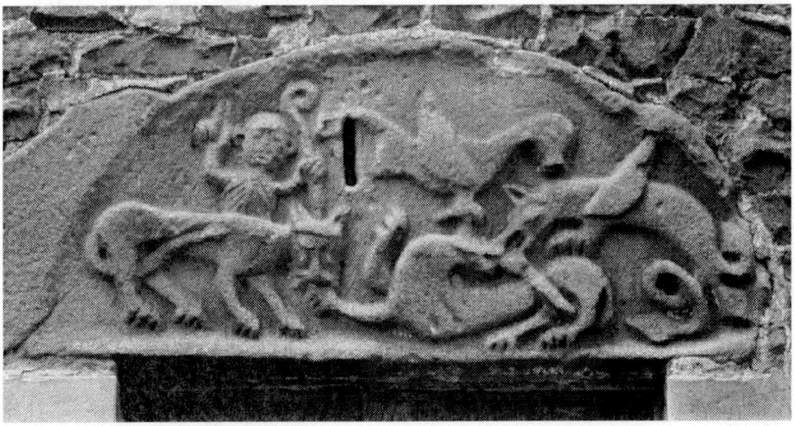

The Romanesque tympanum, Stoney Stanton.

with outstretched wings, and a figure holding a crook. Intriguingly there is a vertical slot through the stone that is perhaps not part of the original carving. The conventional description is of a bishop fighting dragons, but this is neither complete nor entirely accurate.

Pevsner [1960], in his terse style of writing, describes this feature as: 'Norman tympanum now over north doorway of the chancel. A very odd representation. On the left an ox (lamb?) and behind it a bishop with crosier and blessing raised hand. The ox attacks a dragon (is attacked by a dragon?). On the dragon perches an eagle, and from the right a second dragon attacks the first. What is the meaning of this Germanic barbarity?'

Pevsner's derogatory question deserves pondering over but is unlikely to be answered conclusively. We are clearly looking into a mindscape of symbolism far removed from later Christian iconography. For instance, according to Anne Ross [1967], the Celts believed the world to be haunted not by sweet-singing Otherworld birds but by malevolent bird-flocks in the service of hostile gods. Although the Celts predate the carving of this tympanum by some centuries, such beliefs may have lived on as, until comparatively recently, death was thought of as coming in the form of a bird, sometimes a great black screaming night bird. Similarly, until recently ravens were regarded as favourite familiars of witches.

Bear in mind that such tympana would originally not have been bare stone, but covered with a white 'undercoat' and then strongly coloured.

Swithland

St Leonard's church dates to the thirteenth century. In the churchyard are early Swithland slate tombstones and later ones with more elaborate decoration. Many have sentimental epitaphs, such as this:

In memory of Matthew Simpson. 1827
From ling'ring Pains and Time with all its Cares.
By Death releas'd in our declining Years;
Of all our Friends we take a long farewell,
Awhile in these cold silent Graves to dwell:
O may we meet on the celestial Shore,
Where Sickness Pain and Death shall be no more.

Sir Joseph Danvers (1686 to 1753) requested that he be buried with his dog. As this could not be allowed in consecrated land, his tomb is half-in and half-out of the churchyard. On the sides the local

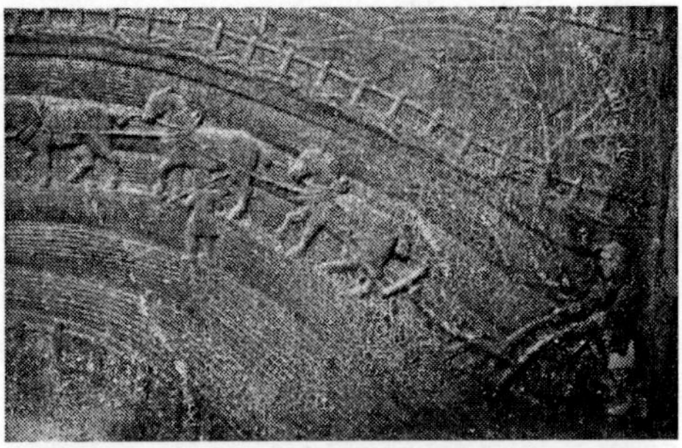

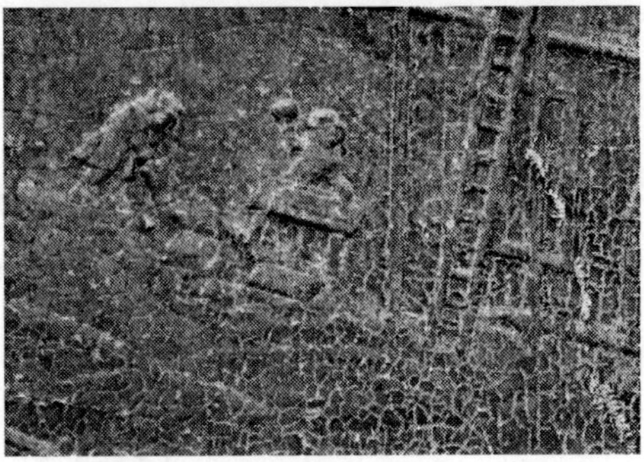

slate has been superbly carved by John Hind into scenes of ploughing, building, a castle, a ship and a church with hills behind (see photographs opposite).

A lantern-headed cross, dated to about 1500, stands in a field behind Swithland Hall (Landranger Ref. 129: 556126). It originally stood in Mountsorrel but was moved in the 1793 by Sir John Danvers, the then owner of Swithland Hall. It its place he erected the domed Butter Market that still stands in Mountsorrel.

Above: *Details of John Danvers' tomb, Swithland*
Below: *Thorpe Arnold font.*

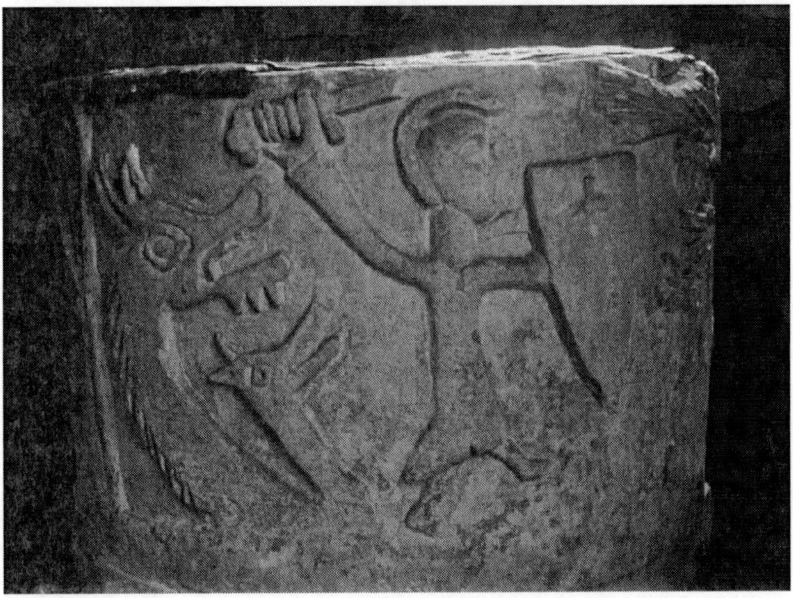

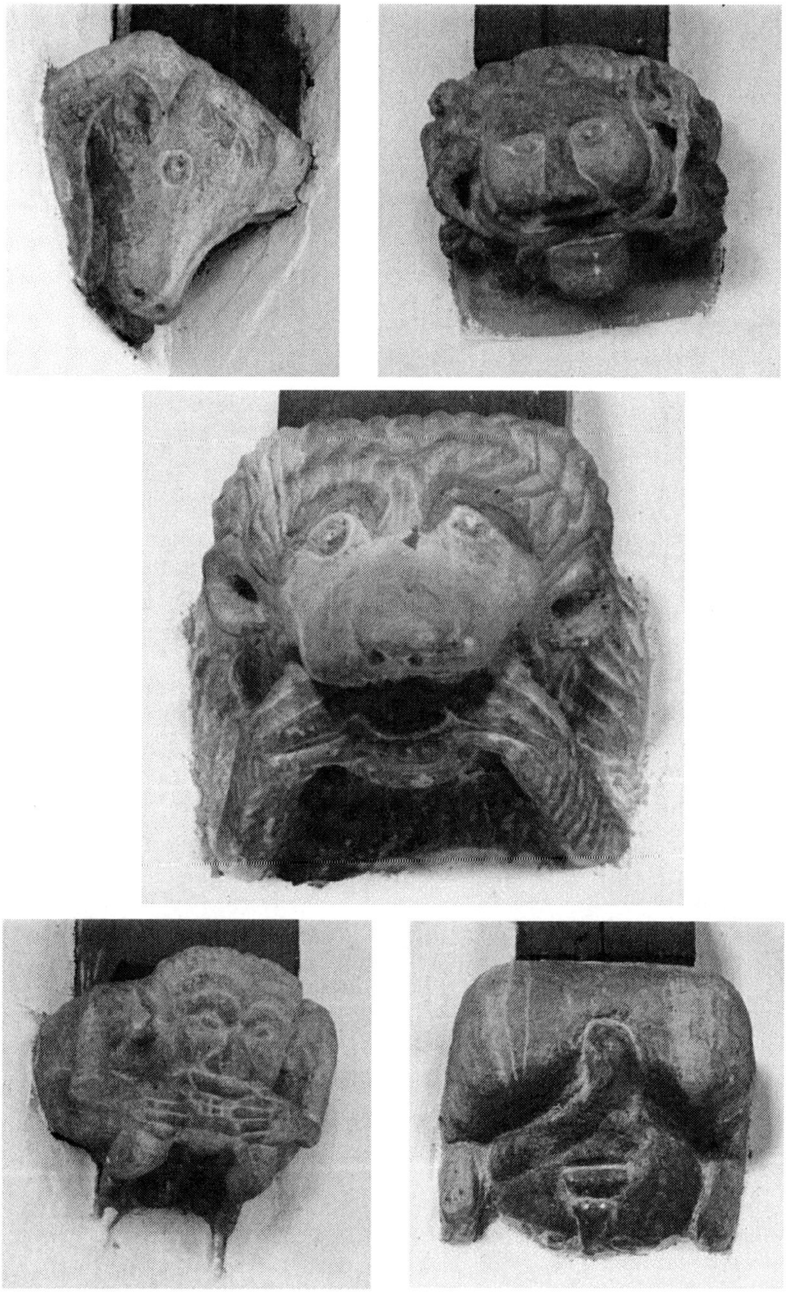

Thorpe Arnold corbels.

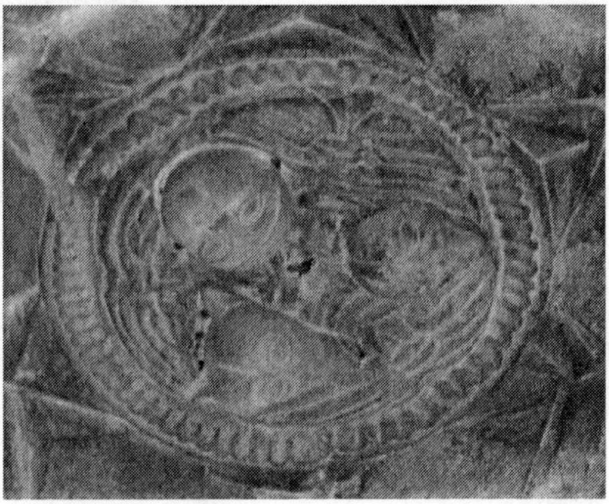

The oldest Romanesque stone boss in Britain in the chancel at Tickencote.

Thorpe Arnold

The Leicestershire church with the most vigorous medieval carving is perhaps St Mary's at Thorpe Arnold (Land- ranger Ref. 129:770201). The Romanesque font depicts a figure fighting five dragons — or are there just two multi-cephalic beasts? (Ipswich church has a stone with a similar depiction of St Michael and a dragon.) In addition, there is a Romanesque capital with two lions' heads (one a tongue-poker) and two human heads.

Even more special is the collection of eight superbly executed corbels in the nave. These carvings presumably date from about 1300, along with most of the rest of the church. They depict two gurning faces (one human, one bestial), a green man, a horned cow,

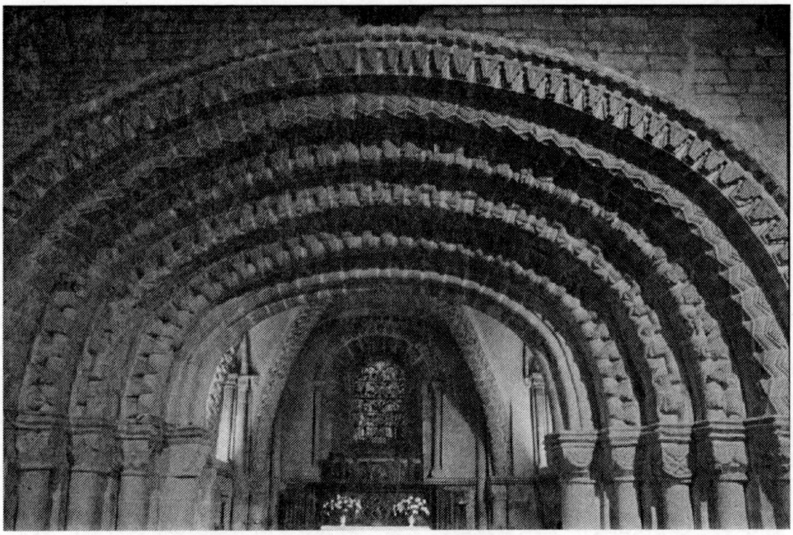

The chancel arch in Tickencote church.

and an ambiguous figure that could be a slightly-disguised male exhibitionist.

Tickencote

St Peter's church (Landranger Ref. 141:990095) was restored in 1792. The west front is less a restoration than a unique blend of eleventh and eighteenth century ideas. The nave is 'mock Norman', although the chancel is a more accurate restoration of the original Romanesque architecture. The chancel roof vaulting is unique in an English parish church and comparable only to that in the choir of Canterbury Cathedral (which was built later in the twelfth century). The boss in the apex incorporates three heads, said to be two muzzled bears and a monk's head. It is probably the oldest Romanesque roof boss in the country.

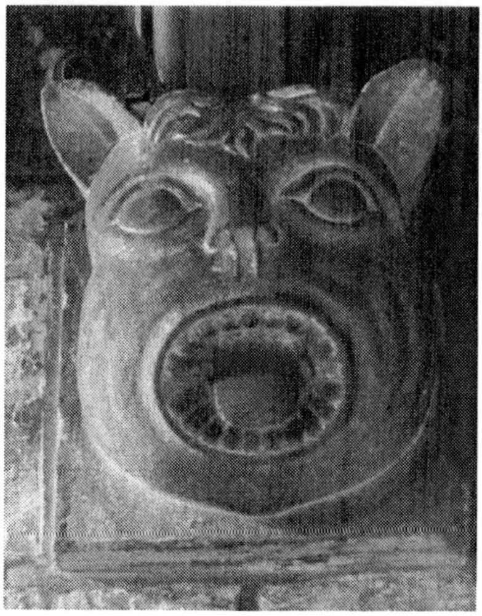

Corbel in the nave of Tickencote church.

The chancel arch is a remarkable example of Romanesque carving, with seven bands of carving, including squared-off foliage, menacing beak heads and green men. It was probably built between 1130 to 1150. It should have been semi-circular but poor construction has caused it to 'slump'.

There are twelve deeply-carved twelfth century corbel heads in the nave, including two tongue-pokers and a green man. The font dates to about 1200 and is decorated with arcades and stylised vegetation, plus human heads on the corners. In the chancel there is an over-life-size oak effigy of a thirteenth century knight.

Tilton on the Hill

Tilton on the Hill is Leicestershire's highest village, at about 215 metres (approx. 660 feet) above sea level. Carved heads abound inside and outside St Peter's church (Landranger Ref. 141:743057). A fine collection of grotesque animals act as gargoyles on the aisles and nave. One appears to be a figure with its head between its legs and what therefore may be a prominent scrotum (this is akin to the ambiguous figure in the nave at Thorpe Arnold). Other figures inside include some faces with curiously asymmetrical features. The

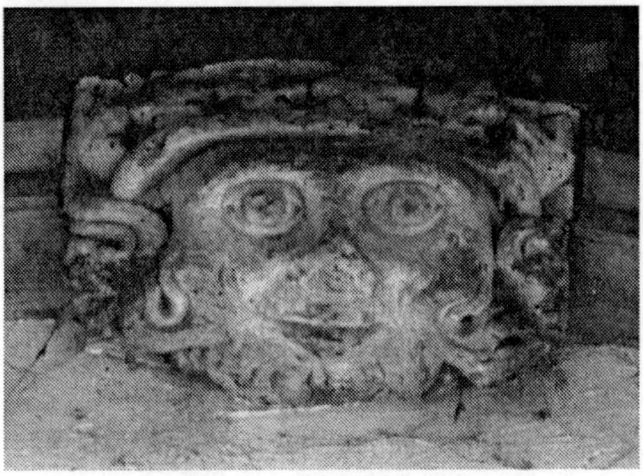

Above: *Tilton roof boss.*
Below: *Whissendine roof boss.*

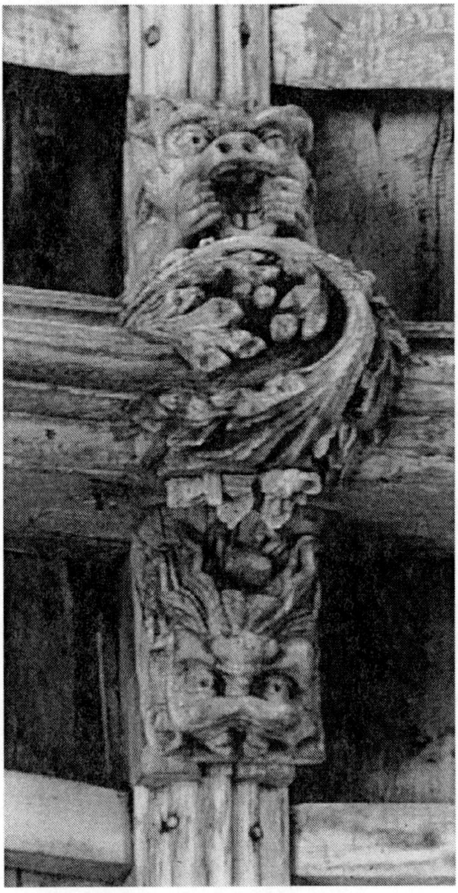

wooden roof bosses include four foliate heads.

Whissendine
St Andrew's church (Landranger Ref. 140: 833143) has thirteenth century north arcade and a fourteenth century south arcade and tower. The transverse arches in the north aisle were added in the fifteenth century to prevent the arcade collapsing under the weight of the high clerestory roof added in the late fifteenth century.

The attractive interior has excellent corbels and arch springers including a tongue-poker. Look out for the heads among the Romanesque stiff leaf in the north aisle arcade.

The wallplates supporting the roof of the nave are decorated with superb wooden figures. The roof is partially fifteenth century but is dated 1728, when it was extensively repaired. There are roof bosses, including a gurning face.

The sixteenth century south aisle screen was originally in St John's College, Cambridge, and removed to Whissendine in 1892, when the church was undergoing restoration.

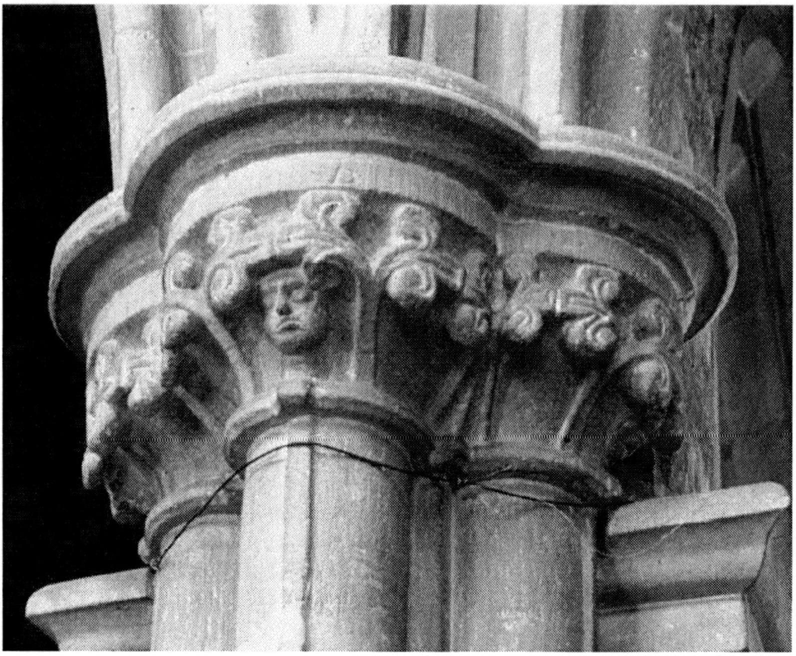

Romanesque capital with stiff leaf and human face, Whissendine.

The font is fourteenth century but seems unfinished on four of the eight sides. The original stone altar slab was restored to its original position in 1892, when it was joined by a reredos and east window from the Kemp studio.

Wymondham

St Peter's is a large, cruciform church with a crypt under the north aisle (Landranger Ref. 130:852186). The tower is thirteenth century, with a late fourteenth or early fifteenth century belfry and arcades. Unusually, the stone altar survives.

On the outside are various small faces in a variety of styles. One of the four gargoyles around the tower, on the south side, is gurning.

Inside the north and south aisles have excellent heads in the arch springers. Also superb are the fourteenth century capitals, which include cows' heads on the north aisle. On the south aisle capitals are unusual demi-angels with vast wings and holding a musical instrument, sun, moon, and other emblems, these are late fourteenth or early fifteenth century.

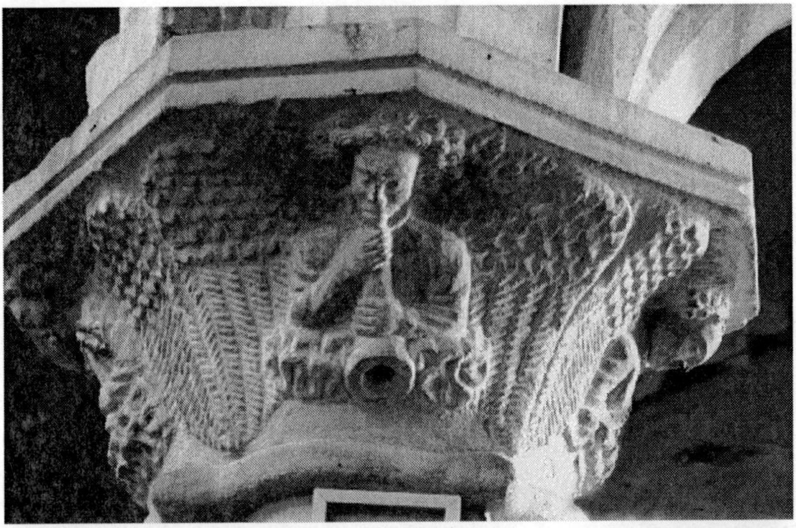

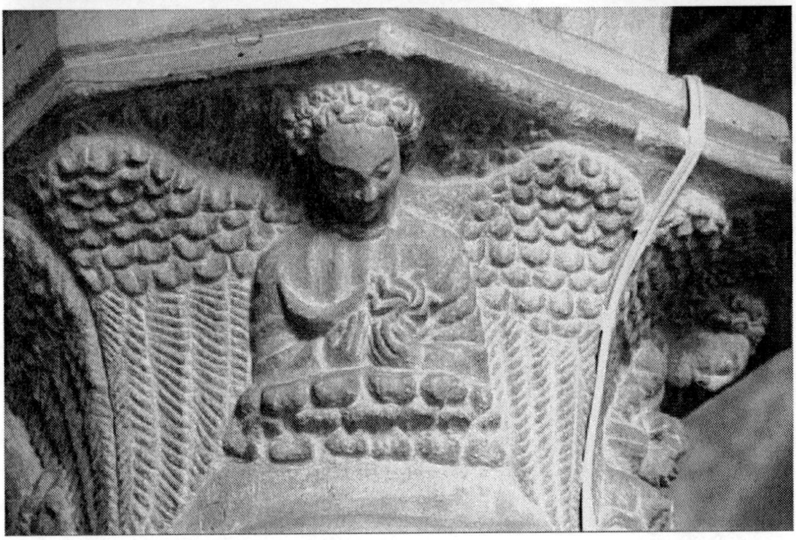

Late fourteenth or early fifteenth century capitals in Wymondham

The thirteenth century effigy is depicted dressed in mail with a frog under the point of the sword, usually interpreted to mean he had fought against the French; an effigy of similar age in St Mary's church at Melton Mowbray also has the same detail, although rather more damaged by the passage of time.

Sources

Apart from the first edition of the *Good Gargoyle Guide* (Trubshaw 1990b) and the subsequent CD-ROM *Interactive Gargoyles and Grotesque Carvings of Leicestershire and Rutland* (Trubshaw 2002), I am not aware of any other attempt to catalogue medieval carvings in Leicestershire and Rutland. The Sites and Monuments Record created and maintained by Leicestershire Museums does include known Anglo-Saxon carvings, but does not attempt to cover the much more extensive later medieval material. Pevsner (1984) makes only occasional references to medieval carvings and omits many of the best examples in the counties.

The list of medieval carvings here does not claim to be complete. My own photographic collection, although depicting many hundreds of examples (only a few of which are reproduced here), is but a small sample of the surviving examples. A comprehensive catalogue of this great wealth of medieval art would require considerable effort but is long overdue.

Selected bibliography of books relating to church carvings

Allen, J. Romilly, 1997, *Norman sculpture and the medieval bestiaries*; reprinted Llanerch Publishers c.1990.

Andersen, Jorgen, 1977, *The witch on the wall: medieval erotic sculpture in the British Isles* Allen and Unwin.

Anderson, M.D., 1938, *Animal carvings in British churches* Cambridge UP.

Anderson M.D., 1967, *The choir stalls of Lincoln Minster* Friends of Lincoln Cathedral.

Anderson, M.D., 1971, *History and imagery in British churches* John Murray.

Anderson, William, 1990, *The Green Man*, HarperCollins.

Andrews, Francis B., 1922, *The medieval mason and his methods*; reprinted Dover 1999.

Andrews, William (ed.) 1892, *Bygone Leicestershire*; reprinted S.R. Publishers 1969.

Bailey, Richard N., 1980, *The Early Christian Church in Leicester and its Region*, Leicester UP.

Bailey, R.N., 1990, *The Meaning of Mercian Sculpture*, University of Leicester Press.

Bailey, Richard N., 1996, *England's earliest sculptors* Pontifical Institute of Medieval Studies.

Bailey, Richard N., 1996, *Ambiguous birds and beasts* Friends of the Whithorn Trust.

Basford, Kathleen, 1977, 'Quest for the Green Man' in *Symbols of power*, H.R. Ellis Davidson (ed), D.S. Brewer.

Basford, Kathleen, 1978, *The Green Man*, D. S. Brewer; reprinted 1996.

Beavitt, Paul, 1995, 'Geophysical and building survey at Launde Abbey' in *Transactions of the Leicestershire Archaeological and Historical Society* Vol. 69 p22–31.

Bechwith, John, 1974, *Early Mediaeval Art*, Thames and Hudson.

Benton, Janetta Rebold, 1997, *Holy terrors —gargoyles on medieval buildings* Abbeville Press.

Betty, J.H., and C.W.G. Taylor, 1982, *Sacred and satiric: medieval stone carving in the West Country* Redcliffe.

Billingsley, John, 1995, 'Archaic heads: guardians of the boundaries', *Mercian Mysteries* No.24.

Billingsley, John, 1998, *Stony gaze: Investigating Celtic and other stone heads*, Capall Bann.

Blackwood, John, 1986, *Oxford's gargoyles and grotesques* Charon Press.

Blackwood, John, 1988, *Windsor Castle's gargoyles and grotesques* Charon Press.

Brandwood, Geoffrey K., 1987, Ancient and modern: Churches and chapels around Market Harborough, Leicestershire Museums.

Brandwood, Geoffrey K., 1990, 'To scrape or not to scrape? Plaster, stucco and Victorian church restorers in Leicestershire' in *Transactions of the Leicestershire Archaeological and Historical Society* Vol. 64 p73–77.

Bridaham, Lester Burbank, 1969, *Gargoyles, chimeres and the grotesque in French Gothic sculpture* Da Capa Press (New York).

Brighton, Christopher, 1985, *Lincoln cathedral cloister bosses* Honywood Press.

Bryce, D., 1989, *Symbolism of the Celtic cross*, Llanerch Enterprises.

Carter, R.O.M., and H.M. Carter,1977, 'The foliate head in England' *Folklore* Vol.78 p269–74.

Cave, C.J.P. , 1948, *Roof-bosses in medieval churches,* Cambridge UP.

Cave, C.J.P., 1951, *Lincoln roof bosses* Friends of Lincoln Cathedral; 2nd ed.

Centerwall, Brandon S., 1997, 'The name of the Green Man', *Folklore* Vol.108 p25–33.

Clapham, A.W., 1928, 'The carved stones at Breedon on the Hill, Leicestershire, and their position in the history of English art' in *Transactions of the Leicestershire Archaeological and Historical Society* Vol. 15, Part 2.

Connelly, Cerridwen, 2001, 'Sile and the head-standing Green Man of Romsey Abbey', *3rd Stone* No.41, pp60–1.

Cross, Joy, 1991, *Imagery in the churches of Nottinghamshire, Derbyshire and Leicestershire* Centre for Local History, University of Nottingham.

Cudmore, Anne, 1994, 'Torture or toothache?' *Countryman* 99iii p64–68 and letters *Countryman* 99v p130

Dawson, Ian, 1988 to 1996, 'Paganism in Essex churches'. Series of articles on medieval carvings in all issues of *Albion's Sacred Heritage* Nos. 1 to 19.

Doel, Fran and Geoff, 2001, *The Green Man in Britain* Tempus.

von Franz, Marie-Louise, 1964, 'The process of individuation' in C.G. Jung (ed.), *Man and his symbols,* Aldus.

Greenhill, F. A., 1958, *The Incised Slabs of Leicestershire and Rutland,* Leicestershire Archaeological and Historical Society,

Greenhill, F. A., 1959, 'Wood-carvings from the nave roof of Market Harborough parish church', *Transactions of the Leicestershire Archaeological and Historical Society,* Vol. 35.

Grimbley, A.E., 1975, 'Church yard crosses', in *Historical notes on the parish of Kirby Bellars,* privately published.

Groesinger, Christa, 1997, *The world upside down: English misericords* Harvey Miller.

Grundy, Thirlie, 1995, *Cry pure, cry pagan in Carlisle cathedral* Thumbprint.

Grundy, Thirlie, 1995, *The misericord carvings in Chester cathedral*Thumbprint.

Grundy, Thirlie, 1995, *The misericord carvings in the cathedral church of St Nicholas, Newcastle upon Tyne* Thumbprint.

Grundy, Thirlie, 1995, *The misericord carvings in the cathedral church of Exeter cathedral* Thumbprint.

Grundy, Thirlie, 1997, *The misericord carver of Hexham Abbey* Thumbprint.

Gurevich, Aron, 1988, *Medieval popular culture: problems of belief and perception* transl. J.M. Bak, Cambridge UP (esp. pxiii-xiv; p132; p176–184)

Harding, Mike, 1998, *A little book of Green Men* Aurum.

Harrison, Alan, 1996, 'The Green Men of Charente [France]' *RILKO Journal* No.48 p15–17.

Harte, Jeremy, 2001, *The Green Man,* Pitkin Unichrome.

Hayward, Anthony, 2002, *The Green Men of Birmingham,* Kiva Publications.

Haward, Birkin, 1999 *Suffolk medieval church roof carvings* Suffolk Institute of Archaeology and History.

Head, Barry, 1980 'The incredible Green Man' *Yorkshire Life* Vol.34 No.9, (Sept) p54–5.

Hicks, Clive, 2000, *A Green Man field guide* Compass.

Hill, Peter, 1996, *In search of the Green Man in Northamptonshire* Orman.

Hutton, Ronald, 1991, *The Pagan Beliefs of the Ancient British Isles,* Blackwell (esp. p314 etc re Green Men).

Hutton, Ronald, 1996, *The stations of the sun* Oxford UP.

Irwin, J., 1988, 'Pillar and cross', *R.I.L.K.O. Newsletter* No.33.

Jackson, Sidney, 1973, *Celtic and other stone heads* privately published.

Jones, Malcolm, 2002, *The secret Middle Ages,* Sutton Publishers.

Judge, Roy, 1979, *The Jack-in-the-Green,* Brewer.

Kahn, Deborah, 1991, *Canterbury Cathedral and its Romanesque sculpture* Harvey Miller.

Kahn, Deborah, 1992, *The Romanesque frieze and its spectator* Harvey Miller.

Kenaan-Kedar, Nurith, 1995, *Marginal sculpture in medieval France* Scolar Press.

Kelly, Eamonn P., 1996, *Sheela-na-gigs: origins and functions* Country House/National Museum of Ireland.

Keyser, Charles, 1927, *A list of Norman tympana and lintels* Elliot Stock (2nd ed).

Lloyd, George, 1960, 'Medieval carved stones at Mold' in *Journal of the Flintshire Historical Society* Vol.18 p164–8.

MacDermott, Mercia, 2003, *Explore Green Men,* Heart of Albion.

McMahon, Joanne, and Jack Roberts, 2001, *The sheela-na-gigs of Ireland and Britain* Mercier Press.

Matthews, John, 2001, *The quest for the Green Man,* Godsfield.

Matthews, Max, 2002, *Sepulchral Effigies in Leicestershire and Rutland,* Heart of Albion Press.

Millar, Ronald, 1997, *The Green Man companion and gazetteer* SB Publications.

Morris, Richard, 1989, *Churches in the Landscape,* J. M. Dent.

NADFAS (National Association of Decorative and Fine Arts Societies), 1989, *Inside Churches,* Capability Publishing.

Negus, Tina, 2003, 'Medieval foliate heads: a photographic study of green men and green beasts in Britain', *Folklore,* Vol. 114, p247–70.

Nichols, John, 1795, *History and Antiquities of the County of Leicester,* Vol I, Part 1; reprinted S.R. Publishers, 1971.

Nichols, John, 1800, *History and Antiquities of the County of Leicester,* Vol III Part 1; reprinted S.R. Publishers, 1971.

Nichols, John, 1804, *History and Antiquities of the County of Leicester,* Vol III Part 2; reprinted S.R. Publishers, 1971.

Nichols, John, 1811a, *History and Antiquities of the County of Leicester,* Vol IV Part 1 ; reprinted S.R. Publishers, 1971.

Nichols, John, 1811b, *History and Antiquities of the County of Leicester,* Vol IV Part 2; reprinted S.R. Publishers, 1971.

Parkin, Gloria, 1989, *Grotesques from Durham Cathedral* Gilesgate Studio.

Paynton, Paul A., 1991, *A Short History Guide to St Andrew's Church Whissendine.*

Pennick, Nigel, 1997, *The Celtic Cross,* Blandford .

Pevsner, Nikolaus (revised by E. Williamson and G. Brandwood), 1984, *Leicestershire and Rutland* (The Buildings of England series), 2nd edn (reprinted with corrections 1998), Penguin.

Phillips, Guy Raglan, 1987, *The Unpolluted God,* Northern Lights.

Raglan, Lady, 1939, 'The Green Man in church architecture', *Folklore* Vol. 50 p35–47.

Rose, Martial, and Julia Hedgecoe, c.1996, *Stories in stone —the medieval roof carvings of Norwich Cathedral* Herbert Press.

Senior, Alan, 1996, 'Masked messengers' *Scottish memories* (December issue) p33–4.

Seward, A.C., 1933–4, 'The Foliage, Flowers and Fruit of Southwell Chapter House', *Proceedings of the Cambridge Antiquarian Society*, Vol. 35.

Sheridan R. and A. Ross, 1975, *Grotesques and Gargoyles*, David and Charles.

Stone, L., 1955, *Sculpture in Britain in the Middle Ages.*

Thompson, F.H. (ed), 1983, *Studies in medieval sculpture* Society of Antiquaries.

Tisdall, M.W., 1998, *God's beasts: Identify and understand animals in church carvings* Charlesfort Press.

Toman, Rolf (ed), 1997, *Romanesque: Architecture, sculpture, painting*, Koenemann.

Trubshaw, R.N., 1990a, *Ancient Crosses of Leicestershire and Rutland*, Heart of Albion Press.

Trubshaw, R.N., 1991b, *Good Gargoyle Guide —Medieval Church Carvings in Leicestershire and Rutland*, Heart of Albion Press.

Trubshaw, R.N., 1991c, *Ancient and Modern Myths of Dragon Slaying Saints*, Heart of Albion Press.

Trubshaw, R.N., 1995, *Little-known Leicestershire and Rutland*, Heart of Albion Press.

Trubshaw, R.N., 1996, 'The Green men of Warmington' *Northamptonshire Local History News* Vol.III No.9 p1–3.

Trubshaw, R.N., 1996, 'The facts and fancies of the foliate face' *At the Edge* No.4 p25–8.

Trubshaw, R.N., 2002, *Interactive Gargoyles and Grotesque Carvings of Leicestershire and Rutland*, Heart of Albion Press (CD-ROM).

Valentine, Dora , 1975, *Church Brasses of Leicestershire*, Vaughan Paper No. 20, University of Leicester.

Vaux, J. H., 1989, *The Canterbury Monsters*, Meresborough Books.

Weir, Anthony and James Jerman, 1986, *Images of lust*, Batsford.

Whitwell, Ben, 1991,'The Green Man: a study' in *Land people and landscape* ed. D. Tyszka, K. Miller and G. Bryant, Lincolnshire Books 1991 (Lincolnshire examples).

Wildridge, T. Tindall, 1899, *The grotesque in church art* William Andrews.

Wildridge, T. Tindall, 1991, *Animals of the church in wood, stone and bronze* Heart of Albion Press; reprint of chapter from *The church treasury*, ed. W. Andrews, 1898.

Wilkins, Joan, 1991, 'The Green Man' *Sussex History* No.31.

Williams, Brian C.J., no date (c.1980), *The Church of St Mary & St Hardulph, Breedon on the Hill, Leicestershire.*

Williamson, Paul, 1995, *Gothic sculpture 1140–1300* Yale UP.

Willsher, Betty, 1996, *The Green Man,* Scottish Local History Journal, Vol. 37.

Wright, Peter Poyntz, 1982, *Hunky punks: a study in Somerset stone carving* Avebury; reprinted Heart of Albion Press 2003.

Wylie, Ruth, 1996, 'The Green Man: variations on a theme', *At the Edge* No.4 p20–4.

About this book

Although I was born and partly brought up in Leicestershire, I did not return to live here until 1986. My interest in various little-known aspects of local history and archaeology led me to explore the villages of Leicestershire and Rutland. While travelling around I began to realise that there was an exceptional wealth of medieval carvings, although there had been effectively no prior interest. This *Good Gargoyle Guide* is an attempt to draw attention to these undeservedly overlooked insights into the medieval era.

Even after about eighteen years of 'church crawling' in this area, there are still many churches in Leicestershire and a few in Rutland that I have yet to visit, so no doubt many more delights await my discovery. The information in this book is based only on churches I have visited and photographed. While there are over 150 photographs in this book, they are only a very small proportion of the number of carvings that survive. This vast wealth of medieval art still awaits a systematic survey.

The origins of this book go back to 1990 and 1991 when a series of four booklets (now out of print) appeared; one of these was called *Good Gargoyle Guide —Medieval Church Carvings in Leciestershire and Rutland.* In 1995 some of this information appeared as a guide book, *Little-known Leicestershire and Rutland.*

The same year Heart of Albion Press pioneered the electronic publication of local history with *Little-known Leicestershire and Rutland —the hypertext,* which provided detailed information on the wells, standing stones, medieval carvings and crosses on a set of five floppy discs. From this evolved a CD-ROM, *Interactive Gargoyles and Grotesque Carvings of Leicestershire and Rutland,* published 2002, which added many more images.

The text and illustrations in this second edition of the *Good Gargoyle Guide* are based on *Interactive Gargoyles and Grotesque Carvings of Leicestershire and Rutland,* although with only about half the number of illustrations on the CD-ROM.

About Heart of Albion Press

Heart of Albion Press was founded by Bob Trubshaw in 1989 to publish booklets on Leicestershire and Rutland local history. The success of these initial publications quickly led to a widening range of titles that explored areas usually ignored by mainstream publishing. So far over 70 books, booklets and disc-based publications have appeared, although about one-third of these are now out of print.

At the end of 1995 Heart of Albion Press took over the remaining stocks of the many Leicestershire local history titles originally published by Jonathan Wilshere.

The complete catalogue was made available on-line early in 1996, making Heart of Albion Press among the first UK publishers to make such information available via the InterNet.

Future publishing projects will extend further into the areas of folklore and mythology, notably with the 'Explore Books' series.

Why 'Heart of Albion'?

The name 'Heart of Albion' draws upon the use of Albion as an ancient poetic name for pre-Roman Britain, probably based on the Latin *albus* ('white') as a reference to the colour of the chalk cliffs on the south coast. As early as the 1st century AD Pliny wrote: *Albion ipsi nomen fuit cum Britanniae vocarentur omnes.*

Albion also features in the poetry of William Blake, suggesting an English Utopia. George McKay in *Senseless Acts of Beauty* (Verso 1996) considers that Albion is the alternative Britain to that of industrialism, privilege and over-mighty government, presumably the same sense drawn upon the the pioneers of the free festival movement in the 1970s who called themselves Albion Free State.

Until the 1974 county boundary changes, Leicestershire was a heart-shaped county and is situated just above the middle of England. The term 'Heart of Albion' was first used, to my knowledge, by Paul Devereux in 1975 as the title of two articles about Leicestershire written for *The Ley Hunter.* As the original intention was for Heart of Albion Press to publish titles about Leicestershire, this seemed an entirely appropriate name, especially as Wymeswold (where Heart of Albion Press is based) is situated in the 'cleft' of the heart-shape.

Also published by Heart of Albion Press

Explore Green Men

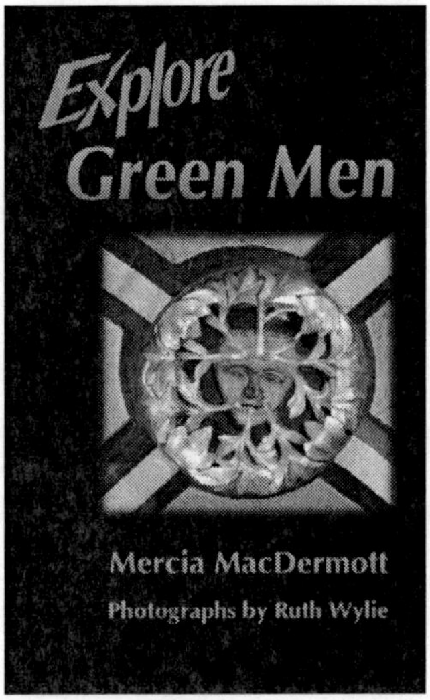

Mercia MacDermott
Photographs by Ruth Wylie

Explore Green Men is the first detailed study of the history of this motif for 25 years. Dr MacDermott's research follows the Green Man back from the previous earliest known examples into its hitherto unrecognised origins in India about 2,300 years ago.

The book starts by discussing the 'paganisation' of Green Men in recent decades, then follows backwards through the Victorian Gothic Revival, Baroque, Rococco and Italianate revivals, to their heyday in the Gothic and the supposed origins in the Romanesque. As part of this discussion there is background information on the cultural changes that affected how Green Men were regarded. The author also discusses the comparisons that have been made with Cernunnus, Robin Hood, Jack-in-the-Green, woodwoses, Baphomet, Al Khidr and Bulgarian *peperuda.* She also investigates which pagan god Green Men supposedly represent.

Explore Green Men is illustrated with 110 photographs and drawings, mostly of Green Men who have never before showed their faces in books.

This book will appeal to all with an interest in Green Men and to art historians looking for a reliable study of this fascinating decorative motif.

ISBN 1 872883 66 4. 2003, perfect bound, demi 8vo (215 x 138 mm), 216 pages, 108 b&w photos, 2 line drawings. **£9.95**

Also published by Heart of Albion Press

Rutland Village by Village

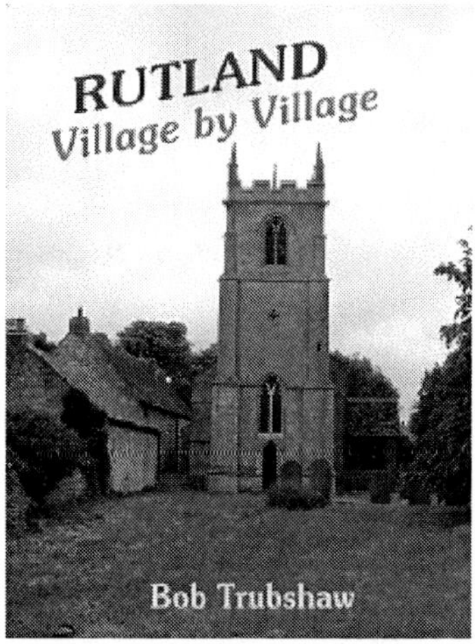

Bob Trubshaw

A guide to the history of all the villages in Rutland, with the emphasis on places that can be seen or visited. Based on the author's sixteen years of research into the little-known aspects of the county.

ISBN 1 872883 69 9. 2003, perfect bound. demi 8vo (215 x 138 mm), 73 + x pages, 53 b&w photos. **£6.95**

Little-Known Leicestershire and Rutland

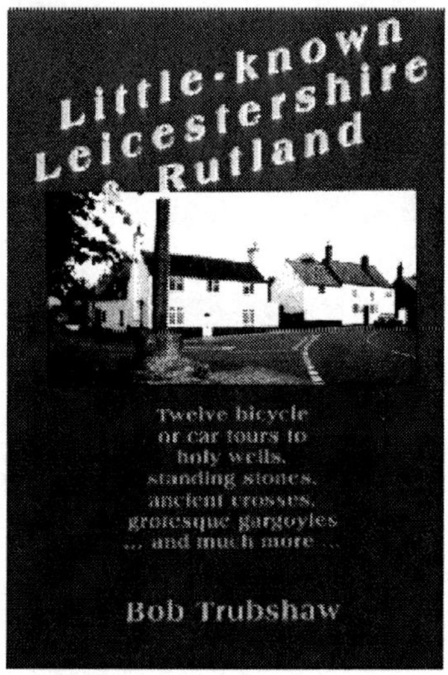

Bob Trubshaw

Drawing upon nearly ten years of research into the holy wells, standing stones, medieval carvings and crosses of the county, this book gives 12 circular bicycle or car routes around unspoiled countryside. Introductory chapters are provided for those less familiar with these topics.

ISBN 1 872 883 40 0. 1995, A5, perfect bound, 128 pages, 9 photos, 14 maps, 49 drawings. **£6.95**

Also published by Heart of Albion Press

Understanding Leicestershire and Rutland Place-Names

Jill Bourne

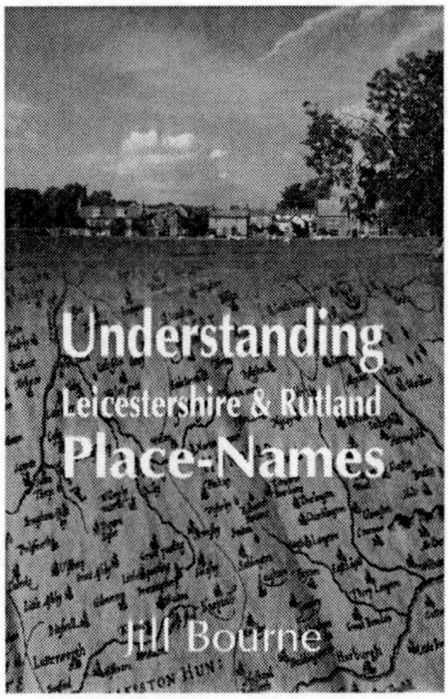

We take for granted the names we use for places. Yet these names are a valuable part of our cultural heritage, providing a detailed insight into the early history of the region. Place-names reveal the otherwise lost voices of our forebears who settled here.

Understanding Leicestershire and Rutland Place-Names analyses the whole range of place-names which occur in Leicestershire and Rutland, most of which were coined between 1,000 and 1,500 years ago. These place-names describe, often in fine detail, the landscape, geology, rivers, buildings, flora, fauna, boundaries, meeting places, roads and track-ways. This book also looks at the distribution of the names, the languages from which they are derived, the successive waves of conquerors and migrants who fought and settled here, and the society they created.

Jill Bourne is an historian, archaeologist and museum professional who has specialised in the area of place-name studies and landscape history for over 20 years.

ISBN 1872883 71 0. 2003, perfect bound. Demi 8vo (215 x 138 mm), 145 + viii pages, 5 maps. **£6.95**

Also published by Heart of Albion Press

Interactive Little-known Leicestershire and Rutland

Text and photographs by Bob Trubshaw

For seventeen years the author has been researching the 'little-known' aspects of Leicestershire and Rutland. Topics include holy wells, standing stones and mark stones, medieval crosses, and a wide variety of Romanesque and medieval figurative carvings - and a healthy quota of 'miscellaneous' sites.

Some of this information appeared in early Heart of Albion publications (mostly long out of print), but this CD-ROM contains extensive further research. The information covers 241 parishes and includes no less than 550 'large format' colour photographs (all previously unpublished).

There are introductory essays, a glossary and plenty of hypertext indexes.

Runs on PCs and Macs.

ISBN 1 872883 53 2. **£14.95** incl. VAT.

Special offer!

Mail order customers save 17.5% (because Heart of Albion is not VAT registered) = **£12.70**

Also published by Heart of Albion Press

Sepulchral Effigies in Leicestershire and Rutland

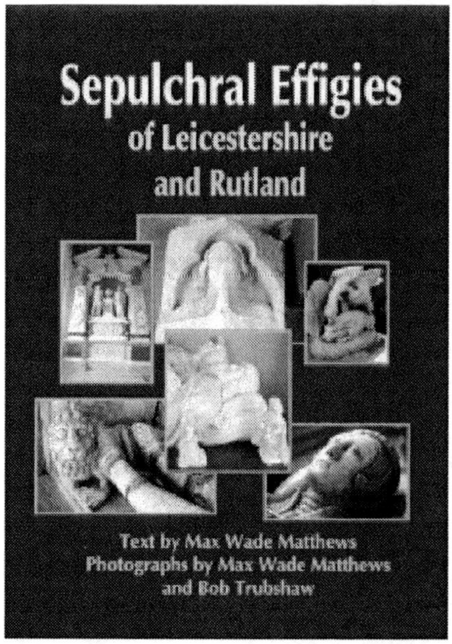

Text by Max Wade Matthews

Photographs by Bob Trubshaw

This CD-ROM makes available for the first time details of the wealth of sepulchral effigies in Leicestershire and Rutland - from thirteenth century priests, thorough alabaster knights in armour and their ladies, to the splendours of seventeenth century Classical aggrandisement. There are even a number of twentieth century effigies too.

350 photos depict 141 effigies in 72 churches, all with detailed descriptions and useful hypertext indexes. Runs on PCs and Macs.

ISBN 1 872883 54 0 **£14.95** incl. VAT.

Special offer!

Mail order customers save 17.5% (because Heart of Albion is not VAT registered) = **£12.70**

Also published by Heart of Albion Press

Hunky Punks
A study in Somerset stone carving

Peter Poyntz-Wright

High up on the famous church towers of Somerset, almost lost to the eye except for their silhouettes, are an amazing series of grotesque stone figures. Carved in the fifteenth and sixteenth centuries, to ornament corners and break up straight sections of masonry, these figures are known in some rural areas at hunky punks.

This book combines a fascinating historical and architectural study with a stunning collection of photographs. Peter Poyntz-Wright's research provides the first thorough account of the hunky punks and gives us a direct insight into the medieval mind. He examines the techniques and influences of the medieval masons, and considers methods of attachment and the effects of weathering.

The author has recorded a host of hitherto unknown and inaccessible medieval carvings the first time —and possibly for the last. They include such creatures as dragons, griffins, hounds, stags, heraldic creatures, a basilisk, the devil, a woman in childhood, and many others. However many of the hunk punks are suffering seriously from the effects of wearing, and some, without costly restoration, may not survive for many more years.

Peter Poyntz-Wright is author of *The Parish Church Towers of Somerset* and *The Rural Bench Ends of Somerset,* and is currently writing a biography of the early sixteenth century Somerset woodcarver, Simon Warman. He lives in Somerset and lectures widely on medieval architectural, biological and historical topics.

ISBN 1 872883 75 X. Spring 2004, A5, perfect bound, approx. 160 pages, 76 full page b&w photos, 3 line drawings. **£9.95**

Also available from Heart of Albion Press

The History and Antiquities of the County of Rutland

James Wright

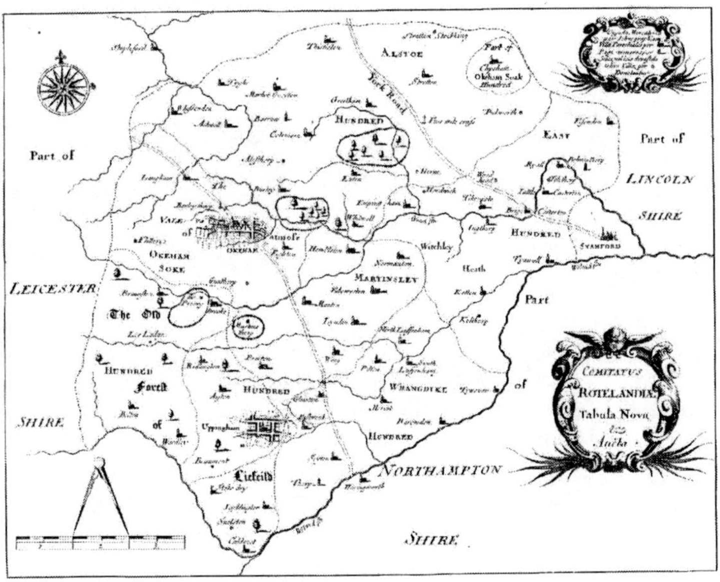

First published in 1684, this pioneering work on local history contains a wealth of information. However copies of the book are hard to come by, so the entire text has been scanned in and made available as high resolution images on this CD-ROM.

Available from Heart of Albion Press for **£10.00.**

Also written by Bob Trubshaw and published by Heart of Albion Press

Explore Mythology

Bob Trubshaw

Myths are usually thought of as something to do with 'traditional cultures'. The study of such 'traditional' myths emphasises their importance in religion, national identity, hero-figures, understanding the origin of the universe, and predictions of an apocalyptic demise. The academic study of myths has done much to fit these ideas into the preconceived ideas of the relevant academics.

Only in recent years have such long-standing assumptions about myths begun to be questioned, opening up whole new ways of thinking about the way such myths define and structure how a society thinks about itself and the 'real world'.

ISBN 1 872883 52 1. 2003, perfect bound, demi 8vo (215x138 mm), 220 + xx pages, 17 line drawings. **£9.95**

Explore Folklore

Bob Trubshaw

There have been fascinating developments in the study of folklore in the last twenty-or-so years, but few books about British folklore and folk customs reflect these exciting new approaches. As a result there is a huge gap between scholarly approaches to folklore studies and 'popular beliefs' about the character and history of British folklore. *Explore Folklore* is the first book to bridge that gap, and to show how much 'folklore' there is in modern day Britain.

ISBN 1 872883 60 5. 2003, perfect bound, demi 8vo (215x138 mm), 196 + xii pages, 4 b&w photos, 4 line drawings. **£9.95**

Full details of current Heart of Albion publications online at www.hoap.co.uk

When ordering by post please add £1.30 towards postage and packing.

To order books or request our current catalogue please contact

Heart of Albion Press
2 Cross Hill Close, Wymeswold
Loughborough, LE12 6UJ

Phone: 01509 880725
Fax: 01509 881715
email: albion@indigogroup.co.uk
Web site: www.hoap.co.uk